WRITING EROT

How To Books on Successful Writing

Copyright & Law for Writers
Creating a Twist in the Tale
Creative Writing
How to Be a Freelance Journalist
How to Publish a Book
How to Publish a Newsletter
How to Start Word Processing
How to Write a Press Release
How to Write & Sell Computer
 Software
How to Write for Television
Making Money from Writing
Mastering Business English
Researching for Writers
Starting to Write
Writing a Nonfiction Book

Writing a Report
Writing a Textbook
Writing an Assignment
Writing an Essay
Writing & Publishing Poetry
Writing & Selling a Novel
Writing Business Letters
Writing Erotic Fiction
Writing for Publication
Writing Pantomime
Writing Reviews
Writing Romantic Fiction
Writing Science Fiction, Fantasy &
 Horror
Writing Short Stories & Articles
Writing Your Dissertation

Other titles in preparation

The How To series now contains more than 200 titles in the
following categories:

Business & Management
Computer Basics
General Reference
Jobs & Careers
Living & Working Abroad

Personal Finance
Self-Development
Small Business
Student Handbooks
Successful Writing

Please send for a free copy of the latest catalogue for full details
(see back cover for address).

SUCCESSFUL WRITING

WRITING EROTIC FICTION

How to write a successful erotic novel

Pamela Rochford

How To Books

Cartoons by Mike Flanagan

British Library Cataloguing-in-Publication data
A catalogue record for this book is available from the British Library.

© Copyright 1998 by Pamela Rochford.

First published by How To Books Ltd, 3 Newtec Place,
Magdalen Road, Oxford OX4 1RE, United Kingdom.
Tel: (01865) 793806. Fax: (01865) 248780.

Note: The material contained in this book is set out in good faith for
general guidance and no liability can be accepted for loss or expense
incurred as a result of relying in particular circumstances on statements
made in the book. The laws and regulations are complex and liable to
change, and readers should check the current position with the relevant
authorities before making personal arrangements.

Produced for How To Books by Deer Park Productions.
Typeset by Kestrel Data, Exeter.
Printed and bound in Great Britain by Cromwell Press,
Trowbridge, Wiltshire.

Contents

List of Illustrations

Preface

Writing an erotic novel is easy, or so a lot of people would have you believe. But sustaining the few pages of erotic fantasy – which just about anyone can write – to the 80,000 words required by most publishers, involving interesting characters and a believable plot (or at least be well written enough to evoke Coleridge's 'willing suspension of disbelief' in the reader) is much harder.

If you're interested in erotic writing and want to learn how to write a novel of your own, this book will show you the difference between romance and erotica, introduce you to the various techniques used in fiction writing, and set you on the right road to writing your own erotic novel.

Black Lace published their hundredth title in August 1997, and have sold over two million copies to date. Virgin and Hodder Headline publish nine erotic titles per month between them, and the smaller presses usually publish one a month. There isn't quite as much competition in this market as there is in romance or crime, so there's more likelihood of having your erotic novel accepted.

The case studies and practical exercises in this book are supported by advice from commissioning editors and successful writers in the genre.

In addition to Elizabeth Coldwell, I would particularly like to thank Kerri Sharp of Black Lace, Mike Bailey of Headline, and Nick Austin of NEL for their valued assistance in the writing of this book and the development of my own erotic style.

I would also like to thank the following editors and authors for their helpful contributions: M. Bernard, Cleo Cordell, Portia da Costa, Eliza Down, Zak Jane Keir, Helen Pisano (Editor, X Libris), Josephine Scott (Editor, Olympia), Mary Tofts, Sarah Veitch, Adrian Wilkins (Editor, Chimera) and Alan York.

Pamela Rochford

Foreword

As the editor of *Forum* magazine and founder member of the Guild of Erotic Writers, I have been dealing with manuscripts of erotic stories and novels for over ten years.

There are a lot of pitfalls in writing erotic novels – it's a lot harder than it looks – but it is a growing market, and one which particularly welcomes new writers, so it is well worth pursuing. A good erotic novel brings pleasure to its readers, and I hope that many of you who read on will soon be joining the ranks of successful authors who produce good, well-written and enjoyable erotic novels.

Elizabeth Coldwell
Editor, *Forum* magazine

1
Getting Started

DEFINING EROTICA

The difficulty of defining erotica

It's quite difficult to define **erotica**. What one person finds erotic is distasteful to another, or a dull read for someone else. Skimming through contemporary collections of erotic writing doesn't help much, either; the Pandora anthology of women's writing includes a piece by Elizabeth David about food – it doesn't even mention sex, but the sensual quality of the writing is obvious.

Establishing a working definition

M. Bernard, a writer of erotica for both sexes, gives the following definition of erotic fiction:

> A story with all that implies – properly constructed plot (with conflict, resolution, climax, denouement), characterisation (which includes mood, atmosphere and accurate background detail) and, possibly, theme.
>
> It has one crucial added element which distinguishes it from the mainstream story: that is, it contains one or more explicitly described sexual encounters which are integral to the plot – and without the encounters and explicit descriptions, the story would be meaningless.
>
> In other words, the eroticism is not something grafted on like an appendage to a story which could exist of its own accord without it, but forms the core, the very *raison d'être* of the events which make up the tale itself.

Understanding what erotic writing is

Erotic writing has three main attributes

1. The writing is heavily based around the senses.

2. The aim of the book or story is to make the reader feel 'turned on'.

3. The scenes contain action which is sexually explicit.

An erotic book for a predominantly female or mixed audience is heavily based around the senses. This means that it should be richly textured in the way that things taste and smell and sound, as well as in descriptions of how things look and feel. It's important that your audience *feels* as though they're experiencing exactly what your lead characters experience, and can identify with your characters.

Because the whole point of the erotic novel is to make the reader feel 'turned on', your book needs to contain sexually explicit scenes, written and structured in a way that makes them part of the plot.

Understanding what erotic writing isn't

Good erotic writing steers clear of three things:

- crudeness
- coyness in the sex scenes
- overuse of humorous interludes.

There is a market for the 'I put my four-letter-word thing in her four-letter-word thing' type of fiction, but it isn't in the top imprints of erotic fiction. For example, the guidelines for Black Lace specifically say that they don't want 'sleaze'. Make sure that you're rude, rather than crude, so that your readers can enjoy the naughtiness of your tale without wincing at the way in which you tell it.

Although the erotic novel should contain explicit sex scenes, these scenes don't necessarily have to be written in explicit language; sometimes it's more erotic to leave bits out. For example, Donne's Elegy 19, *On his mistress going to bed*, is widely recognised as one of the most erotic poems in the English language, but it doesn't once mention his lover's body parts. The analogy can be carried through to modern erotic writing; as top erotic author Portia da Costa says, 'It's possible to write erotica with the least amount of blatant sexual language. The use of understatement and subtlety can be far more subversive – and far more erotic.'

Most erotic writers tend to steer clear of adding humour; editors are not keen on slapstick, 'Carry On' type scripts or the kind of 'Confessions of . . .' books popular in the 1970s. Modern erotic novels deal much more with relationships between the characters. The odd joke is fine, but putting too much humour into the book risks undermining the erotic elements.

UNDERSTANDING THE DIFFERENCE BETWEEN EROTICA AND ROMANCE

Erotica is one of the most difficult genres to write well. It has much in common with romance – but there are also important differences.

Exploring the similarities between erotica and romance

It's escapist fiction
Both erotica and romance can be defined as **escapist literature,** very much based in fantasy worlds with impossibly attractive characters and (often) a happy ending.

It's easy to read and hard to write
Novels in both genres tend to be 'easy reads' – but that doesn't mean that either is easy to write.

It's very easy to write a sex scene (or a less sexually-explicit scene between two characters in a romantic novel), because almost everyone has their favourite fantasy and can describe it. What's difficult is to sustain this sort of writing for the 80,000 words required by the majority of publishers, while making sure that your book has a well-placed plot, believable characters and dialogue, and stays erotic without turning into farce or cliché.

It isn't considered 'proper' literature
Many people won't admit to buying or reading either romance or erotica, because neither is considered to be 'proper' literature. It's worth noting that half a million Black Lace novels were sold in their first year of the imprint, and the two-million mark was reached before their hundredth novel was published in summer 1997 – so there's certainly a large readership out there – and Mills and Boon has a huge market. Before W H Smith's recent re-organisation, two per cent of the books they sold were erotic

fiction, according to *The Author*, the journal of the Society of Authors. People might not admit to *reading* erotica or romance, but they certainly *buy* it.

Erotica as part of the established literary canon

As for erotica not being 'proper' literature – the poems of Ovid, Catullus, Donne, Marvell, Keats and Browning are in the established literary canon, and some of them are decidedly erotic. Similarly, there are erotic interludes in Chaucer and Boccaccio (both standard texts in English literature degree courses), and in the stories and novels of Hardy, Austen, Eliot, Brontë (Emily, Anne or Charlotte – take your pick – all three were considered to have written 'naughty' books, in Victorian times), Lawrence and Nin. It's worth browsing through a copy of one of the many 'literary guides to erotica', to give you a taste of writers from all ages and all cultures. You'll see that there are female writers as well as male, and that there are erotic texts from the Bible and Greek and Roman writers, as well as from the nineteenth and twentieth century.

Genre fiction and personal taste

Still from the 'literary snob' point of view, it's often claimed that all romantic and erotic novels are rubbish. Yes, some of them are dreadful – but equally, some of them are very good. It's the same with all genre fiction – ghost stories, science fiction, detective stories, thrillers, horror. There are always books which you read and think are terrible, and those which you think are brilliant. Someone else might think that your favourite books are terrible, and vice versa. It's all a matter of personal taste. Erotic novels which are full of spanking bore some people, turn off others, and excite yet others.

'Formula' books

It's often said that romantic and erotic novels are written to a 'formula'. For the romantic novel, it's usually:

- boy meets girl
- the attraction is mutual (whether they admit it or not at the start)
- something comes between them (for example, another character or their jobs)
- the conflict is resolved

- and they all live happily ever after.

For erotic novels, the formula is:

- boy meets girl
- they have lots of sex with each other and different people
- and everyone is happy.

If that were true, no-one would buy erotic or romantic novels, because they'd be much too predictable and boring. Yes, the romantic novel will have a happy ending, and the erotic novel will contain lots of sex scenes – but there's more to it than that, as we'll see in the next three chapters.

Exploring the differences between erotica and romance

The treatment of sex
As Black Lace editor Kerri Sharp says, 'Erotica isn't "Mills and Bonk".' There are imprints 'in between' traditional romance and erotica, such as Robinson's *Scarlet* imprint for erotic romance, but the sexual element in romance is much lighter than in erotica. Of course your readers want to use their imagination, but remember why they bought an erotic novel in the first place. If you stay 'outside the bedroom door' in an erotic novel, your readers will feel cheated, whereas readers don't necessarily want to go beyond the bedroom door in a romantic novel.

Interplay of characters
In romantic novels, there may be a 'love triangle', but the key element is the relationship between the hero and the heroine. In erotic novels, on the other hand, readers expect to see a variety of sex scenes, between a variety of characters. If your chapter plan sticks to sex scenes only between your hero and heroine, your editor will ask you to alter the plot to include encounters between your hero and heroine and other characters.

More scope with the plot
Erotic novels are usually around 75,000 to 90,000 words in length (depending on the publisher), whereas romantic novels (at least, for the Mills and Boon market) tend to be around 50,000 to 55,000 words in length. This means that you have at least 20,000 more

words to play with, so you can introduce other elements than just the relationship between the lead characters. You can happily include devices from other genres, such as thrillers or mystery novels or even detective fiction – Virgin, for example, have their 'Crime and Passion' imprint for erotic crime stories.

BUILDING THE ESSENTIAL EROTIC WRITER'S TOOLKIT

Finding somewhere to work
This doesn't have to be the proverbial book-lined study which looks out over a beautiful garden. A corner of the dining room or the kitchen table will do just as well, as long as you're comfortable with your surroundings and have the space to spread out any papers you're using.

Using a typewriter or word-processor
If you prefer to use pen and paper, you can write the whole of your book or story in longhand. As with your surroundings, your method of writing isn't important, as long as you're comfortable with it.

However, publishers and editors only work from a typed manuscript, so your book will eventually have to be typed. Whether you use a typewriter or a computer word-processing program to type your finished manuscript is entirely up to you (and your budget). You certainly don't need to have all the latest programs and gizmos, including a CD-rom, an internet connection and email, in order to write an erotic novel. Sometimes, these can be a hindrance, because you can become side-tracked and end up spending more time browsing through a CD-rom or something on the World Wide Web, rather than writing!

Building up your reference library

A good dictionary
Even if your spelling is excellent, a dictionary can be a useful browsing tool, helping you to come up with a title – or maybe even sparking off an idea.

A thesaurus
This is useful for synonyms, particularly if you have a 'word block'

and tend to overuse certain words. You could also compile your own erotic thesaurus.

A dictionary of sex
This is useful for browsing and sparking off ideas. Wordsworth publishes a good one.

A sex manual
Again, this is useful for browsing and sparking off ideas. If you have a computer with a CD-rom, you could consider buying the CD-rom version of manuals such as those by Alex Comfort and Anne Hooper.

A book of first names
This is useful for naming characters – a random dip is often the most helpful.

A telephone directory
This is useful for characters' surnames – again, a random dip is often the most helpful.

An atlas of Britain
This is useful on two counts:

● for characters' surnames
● for settings.
   If you're using an actual place, be careful to get the details correct – for example, there are no motorways in Norfolk, and the M11 does not go through Yorkshire.
   If you're using a fictional town, an atlas will help you to avoid using real place names in your chosen county.

A map of the London underground
Again, this is useful for settings. If your novel is set in London and your characters use the tube, make sure that your details are correct: for example, don't say that Islington is on the District line.

LOOKING AT THE MARKET FOR EROTIC NOVELS

Once you've decided that you're going to write an erotic novel, you need to decide on your target audience. There are various

Publisher, contact, address	Required length	Audience	Comments
Black Lace *Editor: Kerri Sharp* Virgin Publishing Ltd 332 Ladbroke Grove London W10 5AH	75–80,000 words	Female	Very detailed and helpful guidelines available
Chimera Publishing *Editor: Adrian Wilkins* PO Box 152 Waterlooville Hants PO8 9FS	75–80,000 words	Mixed	Prefers dominant male subject – don't overdo the corporal punishment (CP) elements
Headline *Editor: Mike Bailey* 338 Euston Road London NW1 3BH	75–80,000 words	Headline Liaisons – mixed Headline Delta – predominantly male	Editor dislikes 'golden rain' scenes
NEL *Editor: Jon Wood* 338 Euston Road London NW1 3BH	90,000 words	Predominantly male	
Nexus *Editor: Peter Darvill-Evans* Virgin Publishing Ltd 332 Ladbroke Grove London W10 5AH	75–80,000 words	Predominantly male	
Olympia Publishing *Editor: Josephine Scott* 36 Union Street Ryde Isle of Wight PO33 2LE		Mixed	Heavy SM – don't send lightweight erotica
X Libris *Editor: Helen Pisano* Little, Brown & Co Brettenham House Lancaster Place London WC2E 7EN	60,000 words	Female	Not keen on heavy SM

Fig. 1. UK publishers currently accepting erotica.

imprints on the market, and all have different audiences and different styles. You need to tailor your writing to fit your particular audience and market.

Choosing your publisher
The main publishers in the erotic market are listed in Figure 1 on page 20. There are other imprints which no longer exist (for example, Penguin's Signet and Robinson's Raven were both 'erotic horror' imprints which were withdrawn in 1997, and Titan's 'Eros' no longer publish erotic novels, concentrating on short stories instead), and there are also small presses around the country which publish erotic novels from time to time.

Keeping in touch with the market
The best way to keep in touch with the market – particularly to find out which publisher is launching a new imprint, which imprints are being withdrawn, and whether there are any major changes to guidelines from the big players – is to subscribe to a magazine dealing specifically with writing and markets in publishing (such as *Writers News*) or to join a group such as the Guild of Erotic Writers, which has access to this kind of information and will pass it on to its readers and members.

Targeting your publisher
Bearing in mind that each imprint has a different target market, you need to decide which publisher you want to target *before* you write your novel. Read a few novels (by different authors) in your chosen imprint. If you don't enjoy them, then pick another imprint and read a few more books. This will give you an idea of the kind of manuscripts that the publisher is looking for. If you're not sure which authors to pick, ring the editorial department and ask them which authors or titles are their most popular. These are the kind of books that the publishers know sell well – and they're likely to be more sympathetic to submissions in these veins.

Applying for guidelines
Once you've decided on your chosen publisher, write to the editor and ask for a copy of their contributors' guidelines – don't forget to enclose an SAE. Once you've read the guidelines, start to write your novel, and always keep those guidelines in mind. There's no point in writing a 90,000-word novel for X Libris, or a

60,000-word novel for Black Lace, because the former will be 30,000 words too long, and the latter will be 20,000 words too short. And sending a 'vanilla' erotic novel to Olympia will guarantee a rejection, because they cater for a heavy SM (sadism and masochism) market. Similarly, X Libris is not likely to accept a heavy SM novel.

Knowing your audience

Figure 1 also shows the kind of audience for each imprint. There is a difference between writing for women, writing for men, and writing for a mixed audience, in the kind of topics covered, the language used, and the general style of writing.

Don't patronise your readers

Your readers want an erotic read, but that doesn't mean that they're poorly-educated and can be fobbed off with a plot which consists of a series of bonks, the kind of dialogue found in second-rate sleazy films, or cardboard and stereotyped characters. Your readers are looking for a book with a good (and reasonably intricate) plot, intelligent dialogue, and interesting characters. And they want it to be erotic, as well – after all, that's why they chose to read an erotic novel or story in the first place.

Remember that men and women like different things

Kerri Sharp, editor of Black Lace, says, 'The female erotic imagination is more diffuse than obsessive. Women are more interested in scenarios, the environment and the dynamics between the characters; men put a lot more emphasis on anatomy.' If you're writing for a female or a mixed audience, make sure that you describe the setting and the emotions as well as any sexual action.

Taking advice from the horse's mouth

It's helpful to have a person in mind when you're writing. If you're writing for one of the women-oriented publishers, imagine that a female friend or partner is your target audience; if for a male audience, think of a male friend or partner; and if you're writing for a mixed audience, imagine that a close male friend or partner is your audience, as well as a female friend or partner. What do they enjoy about erotic novels? What do they wish there was more of? What do they wish that writers would leave out? Feedback of this kind is very useful in helping you to structure your novel.

ANALYSING YOUR OWN WRITING

Think about why you want to write erotica

Before you analyse your writing itself, think about why you've chosen to write erotica.

Making money

If you're doing it just to make money, you could be setting yourself up for disappointment. Newspapers and magazines often print articles about publishers paying six-figure advances for first novels – but those kind of advances are very rare, and they're non-existent in the erotica market, where the advance for a first novel might be less than a thousand pounds.

Although you may eventually be able to make a living out of writing erotic novels, remember that it takes time to become established. And remember, too, that although there are several publishers in the market, there are also a lot of good writers out there, so competition is fierce.

Writing for pleasure

If, on the other hand, you've chosen to write erotica because you enjoy reading it, and you'd like to write the kind of fiction that you enjoy, then you have a much better chance of writing good erotic novels, and being paid for them.

Ask a friend for honest criticism

If you have someone in mind when you're writing your novel, ask him or her to read your manuscript and give you honest comments. What did he or she like most about it? What didn't he or she like about it?

The important thing is that your 'audience of one' *must* be honest, telling you where the dialogue or plot or characterisation needs improving, as well as giving you praise. 'Oh, it's really good, I loved it,' will do you more harm than good – you might send off work to an editor which really isn't up to scratch.

Constructive criticism

Constructive criticism, on the other hand, can turn a promising manuscript into a well-written and enjoyable book – not to mention saving you some rejection letters and a lot of heartache. 'Yes, I enjoyed it,' tempered by, 'but I wasn't sure about your plot,' might hurt at the time – but it will help you much more, because your revision will make the manuscript better.

Be honest with yourself

If you can, go through a few pages of your writing objectively. What are your weak points? What are your strong points?

Use the following checklist to help pinpoint your strong and weak areas.

Technical points

- spelling

- punctuation – particularly use of commas, apostrophes, semi-colons and speech-marks

- grammar – particularly tenses (don't mix them!) and use of adverbs/adjectives

- paragraphing – length, correct usage (particularly regarding dialogue)

See the section on grammar in Chapter 2 for further details.

Dialogue

- Is your dialogue realistic and natural?

- Does your dialogue add something to the plot?

- Are you guilty of **throat-clearing** (*ie* making your characters say 'mm,' 'oh' or 'well', which acts as padding rather than adding to the plot or characterisation)?

Characters

- Can your reader *see* your characters – *ie* have you described them adequately?

- Are your characters consistent?

Plot

- Is your plot too simple or too complex?

- Are your characters 'doing' enough (*ie* have you made sure that your characters are not spending too much time reflecting or thinking – soliloquies are not erotic)?

CHECKLIST

- Read widely in your chosen imprint. Think about whether you enjoyed reading the books, and what you liked most and least about the novels.

- Make sure that you have an up-to-date copy of the editor's guidelines. If your copy is six months old, it's worth checking again in case there have been any changes.

- Think about whether you are comfortable with the style of writing in your chosen market. If not, choose another imprint – or review whether you'd be better suited to writing in a different genre.

- Can you see any similarities between the books you've read? Look at the tone, the style and the way the books are structured. Are there any recurring themes? What kind of characters is the author writing about? How does the author balance the sexual content of the book with the rest of the plot?

CASE STUDIES

Anna checks things out

Anna works in a large office, writing the company newsletter and press releases. She has an excellent grasp of English and knows how to write good features. She'd like to write an erotic novel for women and has written several rejected romances – the rejection slips being because her sex scenes are too steamy and the conflict between her characters isn't strong enough. She has read widely in her chosen market and has written to the editors, asking for their guidelines. She feels that she is now in a good position to start writing her own novel.

Bill sets himself up for rejection

Bill has also read several erotic novels. He thinks that the ones he's read are hopeless, and believes that he can do a lot better. He hasn't bothered sending for any guidelines and is shocked when the manuscript he submits is rejected for being too short and including scenes which the editor has said are unacceptable.

ASSIGNMENT

From the list of publishers in Figure 1, decide which imprint is the one which you would most like to write for. Read at least three novels by different authors and analyse them (use the final checklist point above to help you analyse them). Once you're sure that this is the market you want to work in, apply for the editor's guidelines.

2
Putting it into Words

ANALYSING THE ELEMENTS OF AN EROTIC NOVEL

The erotic tale has exactly the same elements as mainstream fiction. You need:

- an interesting plot
- well-drawn and believable characters
- an evocative setting.

But in addition, you also need:

- good, explicit sex scenes.

Above all, remember that if you don't enjoy writing the book, your audience won't enjoy reading it, because your discomfort with the material will be visible in your writing.

The elements of plot, character, dialogue, setting and the sex scene are covered in the following chapters. What links these elements in your book are the words you use, and the way you use them: in other words, grammar (including spelling) and language (including vocabulary).

LOOKING AT GRAMMAR

The building-blocks of your novel

The words you use and the way in which you use them are the **building-blocks** of your novel. Think of your book as being like a house. If you went to view a house and the windows were crooked, there were gaps in the floorboards, the doors wouldn't shut, the light switches and power points were inaccessible, and the bath was set in the middle of the kitchen, you wouldn't buy

27

it. You might not mind the colour of the walls (which you could change quickly and easily), but major flaws would put you off.

The editor's viewpoint
Your book is the same. Editors forgive the occasional spelling mistake, typing mistake – spell-check programs don't always pick these up – and grammatical error, but you're not doing yourself any favours if you submit a manuscript full of spelling mistakes and basic grammatical errors.

Your idea might be fabulous, but if your manuscript is badly written, it's unlikely to be accepted. Apart from the fact that sub-literate manuscripts are one of many editors' pet hates, editors just don't have the time to sit there making corrections. They work to a cost basis, so they can't afford to employ freelance editors to rewrite your book to the required standard, either.

Knowing your weak spots
At the same time, not everyone's perfect when it comes to grammar and spelling. if you know that this is your weak spot, invest in a good grammar guide – there are several on the market – and a bad speller's dictionary. Or you could ask a friend who's good at spelling or grammar to read through your manuscript and point out any mistakes you've made.

Some of the points below may seem glaringly obvious; however, these are things that crop up so often in manuscripts submitted to editors that it's worth revising your own writing to check that you haven't slipped into bad habits.

Punctuation – usage and abusage

Apostrophes
Apostrophes are used for

- *belonging to* – for example, 'Peter's ball' or 'the cat's whiskers' (but don't forget, 'the dog wagged its tail', not 'the dog wagged it's tail')

- *a missing letter* – for example, can't (cannot), it's (it is), there's (there is), you're (you are).

Apostrophes are *not* used for

- *plurals* – for example, 'he picked a bunch of daisy's' should be 'he picked a bunch of daisies'.

Commas
Commas are used

- *to mark clauses* (*ie* the words between the commas could be left out, if you wanted to, and the sentence would still make sense). Think of them as breathing spaces. Try reading a long sentence without commas, and you'll soon run out of breath; where you would naturally want to pause is probably where a comma should be to break up the sentence.

Commas are not used

- *to mark adverbs* – for example, in ' "Hello," Peter said, brightly', there should not be a comma after 'said'.

Semi-colons
A semi-colon (;) is used

- *to link two sentences* – for example: 'It was a hot day; Jane was grateful for the fan on her desk.'

- *to punctuate a list of items* – for example: 'Susan checked the ingredients on her list. Raspberries; strawberries; blueberries; blackcurrants; day-old bread; sugar and kirsch. Yes, she had everything she needed to make the summer pudding.'

Dashes and colons
Dashes (–) and colons (:) usually indicate pauses which are stronger than a comma, but not as strong as a full stop, for example: 'I could meet you there – say, at ten?' or 'She wondered if he'd fit in the passenger seat of her Mini: he was taller than she'd expected.'

Exclamation marks
You shouldn't need to use exclamation marks outside dialogue, except possibly for characters' thoughts. Within dialogue or characters' thoughts, use them sparingly, otherwise they soon

become irritating. Journalists and advertising copywriters refer to exclamation marks as 'screamers': *ie* they're used to make a very loud point.

Also, don't use more than one. Otherwise it's non-standard punctuation!! Which editors don't like!!! And it starts to look childish!!!!

Punctuating within speech-marks

- If you continue the sentence after the speech, you need a comma before the closing speech-marks. For example: ' "Hello, I'm Jane," she said, holding out her hand.'

- If you don't continue the sentence after the speech, you need a full stop before the closing speech-marks. For example: '"You must be joking." She stared angrily at him.'

- Use a capital letter inside the speech-marks when the dialogue is the start of a sentence, and a lower case letter if it's a continuation of the sentence. For example: ' "Phew," she said, fanning herself, "isn't it hot, today?" ' or ' "I'm fed up!" she shouted. "My computer's gone wrong, yet again." '

Character's thoughts
These are always written without speech-marks, and not in italics. For example: 'Jane glanced at her watch. I've been waiting for nearly half an hour, she thought. It was obvious that Peter wasn't going to turn up.'

Using italics
The guidelines should tell you when to use italics. Check with your editor – but usually, italics are used for:

- emphasised words (but be careful not to overdo this – your dialogue shouldn't need italics, as the emphasis should speak for itself)

- extracts from letters

- quotes from poems or songs (remember the laws of copyright, here – and you'll be responsible for obtaining and paying for permission to use those quotes)

● titles of books, songs, plays or poems.

Tenses
Always use the past tense – he did, she was doing, they had done – and third person narrative (he and she, rather than I or we). Present tense and first person narrative are not really suited to the erotic novel, unless it's within dialogue – for example when one character fantasies aloud to another.

Make sure that you don't mix your tenses. If you want the character to have a flashback, to show your readers the motivation or background for a particular character, make sure that the flashback starts in a new paragraph. When the flashback ends, you need another new paragraph.

Be careful of your tenses within the flashback, if you use the device. It's very easy to slip from 'he had done something' to 'then he did something else', which confuses your reader.

Starting sentences with conjunctions
Starting a sentence with 'and', 'but' or 'or' is perfectly acceptable nowadays – but be careful how you do it. For example, in 'He ordered fish. And chips'. '– unless you're making the point that your character didn't usually order chips, this should all be one sentence. Remember, sentences usually need verbs, and if you start every sentence with 'and' or 'but', your writing will become very stale, very quickly.

Ending sentences with prepositions
Some editors are fussy about this, some less so. For example, supposing that one of your characters says that she lives with a colleague. She could say, 'My friend, who I live with' – which is colloquial, though not grammatically correct. She could equally say, 'My friend, with whom I live' – which is grammatically correct, but sounds too forced for modern dialogue. Start with the grammatically correct version of your sentence; but if it sounds forced or false in the context of your work, then use the colloquial version.

CHECKING YOUR SPELLING

Some of these mistakes may seem very obvious, but again they
are very common in manuscripts submitted to (and rejected by)
editors.

Looking at commonly misspelt words

The practice of practising . . .
For a verb ending in SE (eg practise, license) – when using it as a
verb, spell it with an S, and when using it as a noun, spell it with
a C. For example, 'Peter **practised** the flute. Then he went to cricket
practice.'

Commonly mixed-up words

● affect and effect
—you have an **effect** upon something, or you **affect** it

● compliment and complement
—compliment means 'to say something nice to someone', *eg* 'he
complimented her on her new dress'
—complement means 'to go well with something', *eg* 'the wine
complemented the chicken'

● dependent and dependant
—a **dependant** (noun) is someone who depends financially upon
you (*eg* a child, an elderly relative); in which case he or she is a
dependent (adjective) person.

● it's and its
—its means 'belonging to it', *eg* 'the dog wagged **its** tail'
—it's means 'it is' or 'it has' *eg* '**it's** a pity that the tennis was
rained off' or '**it's** been sunny all day'

● taut and taught (This one is peculiar to erotic writing.)
—taut meant 'tight', as in 'her nerves were as **taut** as a bow-string'
taught is the past participle of 'teach', as in 'she **taught** French for
a living'

● there, they're and their

—there means a place, as in 'over **there**' or '**there** is a cat sitting on the windowsill'

—they're means 'they are', as in '**they're** going to the beach today'

—their means 'belonging to them', as in 'they put **their** shopping in the boot of the car'

- your and you're

—your means 'belonging to you', *eg* 'is that **your** car?'

—you're means 'you are', *eg* '**you're** very tall'.

LOOKING AT LANGUAGE

Using description to show your readers what's happening

As with any fiction, your erotic novel needs to be descriptive. You may know what your characters look and sound like, in your head, but your reader doesn't. Unless you describe them, your readers won't be able to see your characters, and how they speak and act. What do your characters look like? What are their mannerisms? Do they plod along sedately, or bustle around getting things done?

Using – and overusing – adjectives and adverbs

Don't overdo the adjectives and adverbs, though. For example, in the sentence '"I'm tired," she said wearily,' the word 'wearily' is redundant. If you really need to convey just how weary your character is, describe her actions – for example, does she throw herself into a chair, or flop onto the sofa and rake her hands through her hair as she closes her eyes? Think about what you're trying to say, and the most effective way you can convey it to your readers. Less is more.

Dialogue

Similarly, in dialogue, you don't need to follow every single speech with a verb and an adverb. The following piece of dialogue would be blue-penned very heavily by an editor; the overuse of adverbs makes the dialogue sluggish.

'Hello,' Peter said brightly. 'I'm Peter.'

'Hello. I'm Jane,' Jane said happily.

'Shall we go and sit down?' Peter asked enquiringly.

'Yes. Lets,' Jane said enthusiastically.

Historical settings

Historical settings create their own difficulty. If you've been reading up on Victorian slang and your novel is set in Victorian times, it's very tempting to use your new-found knowledge. However, will your readers be able to follow you? The likelihood is that they won't – unless they happen to have specialised in Victorian studies, in which case they'll also be much less tolerant of any slips you may have made. At the same time, modern slang simply won't fit historical settings. Try to steer a middle course.

ANALYSING VOCABULARY

Expletive deleted

Just because you're writing erotica, it doesn't mean that you have to pepper your work with expletives. Apart from the fact that your editor will probably delete half of them, a novel which is full of monotonous and crude words is, quite simply, boring. Don't limit yourself to a small vocabulary. Use a variety of phrases, particularly for description of bodily parts. Though beware of going so far over the top that you descend into farce – the 'purple-headed womb warrior' or 'mauve banana' belong more to the world of *Viz* than to the world of erotica!

The taboo areas

There are taboo areas, of course: words which people dislike. That isn't just the 'obscene' words – most women, for example, won't respond that well to the idea of a man's penis 'ramming' into a woman, although some men will find it acceptable. The vocabulary you use will depend on your target audience.

A rule of thumb is personal taste: use the words you're comfortable with. For example, if you don't like a particular word, use a synonym. At the same time, beware of being coy. Remember, you're working in a sexually-explicit genre; you don't have to limit yourself to 'his manhood', 'his male hardness', 'her womanhood' or 'her secret centre of pleasure', which have more of a place in romance than in erotica.

Beating the word-block

It's very easy to have a word-block, or find yourself overusing one particular phrase. Ask a good friend to read your work, to spot if you're overusing a phrase – or, if you're using a word-processor, and you suspect that you have a habit of overusing a particular word or phrase, use the 'find and replace' function of the word-processor to check how often you've used it.

Compiling a personal thesaurus
Try making a personal **erotic thesaurus**, culled from the books you read and your own imagination. Make lists for various parts of the body, the sexual act, and orgasm/ejaculation. It takes time, but it will pay dividends – next time you realise that you have a word-block, at least you'll have a couple of other phrases you can use instead.

CHECKLIST

Look at a piece of your writing and check it for the following, using the notes above to help you.

● The accuracy of your punctuation – it's very easy to fall into sloppy habits.

● The accuracy of your spelling. The quickest way to do this is through a spell-check program on a word-processor; if you don't have access to one, ask a friend or local college.

● Whether your vocabulary is 'erotic' – if you haven't already compiled your personal erotic thesaurus, do it now and see how many different words you can find.

● How descriptive your writing is – can anyone else see exactly what you had in mind when you wrote the piece?

● Your use of adverbs and adjectives – think of it as seasoning. Too many will spoil your 'dish', or novel.

CASE STUDIES

Caroline works it out
Caroline reads a lot of erotic novels and would like to write one herself. She was good at writing stories at school, but that was a

long time ago. She knows that her spelling could be better, so she buys a bad speller's dictionary. This helps her feel more confident about tackling her first novel.

Denise doesn't bother

Denise is full of good ideas. She has no problem with finding a plot or keeping the story going for the required number of words. However, her punctuation is erratic and she has particular problems knowing when to use new paragraphs. She submits a synopsis and the first three chapters to an editor; the editor likes the basic idea, but knows that copy-editing the book to the required standard will push the production budget over the limit. Denise's book is rejected.

ASSIGNMENT

Punctuate the following passage correctly, including paragraphing where necessary. Answers are on page 118.

I cant believe its so hot today Jennifer said reclining on the blanket and stretching The weather man did say that it was going to be nearly 30 degrees – the hottest day of the year Sally reminded her friend Yes Jennifer mopped her face with a tissue and pushed her dark hair back from her face But I havent trusted weather forecasts since we held that barbecue last year It was supposed to be sunny and it rained buckets remember Never mind This Sally told her pouring a glass of pinot noir rosé and handing it to her will make you feel a bit better Jennifer accepted the wine Whatd make me feel better is having our own private swimming pool With Fox Mulder as the lifeguard Sally added a look of sheer lust brightening her eyes Jennifer pulled a face That's highly likely isnt it About as likely as fitting a swimming pool into our back garden Sally retorted eyeing the narrow courtyard

3
Structuring the Novel

USING KIPLING'S HONEST SERVING MEN

To continue the analogy of the previous chapter, language and grammar are the building blocks of your novel. However, you need an overall plan or structure to work to – otherwise your novel risks being like a house which has the doors and windows in the wrong places, the porch where the roof should be, and the roof where the floor should be.

Starting a structure

So how should you start to structure your novel? Kipling had a small rhyme about it:

> I have six honest serving men
> They taught me all I know
> Their names are what and why and when
> And who and where and how.

This is true for all fiction, including erotic fiction. The reader wants to know the following:

- *What* is happening? This is the book's action.

- *Where and when* is it happening? This is the book's setting – in time as well as place.

- *Who is* it happening to? These are your characters.

- *Why* is it happening? This is the motivation of your characters and your book's plot.

●   The *how*, of course, is how you tell it to your readers.

Remember, a number of sex scenes placed one after the other doesn't make a plot, or even a structure: it's like having your building blocks without cement. One turn of the page, one yawn from your reader, and the whole lot falls down. As top author Cleo Cordell says, 'There has to be something more than a string of sex scenes and no other content.' Otherwise, what gives your reader the motivation to read on?

You have between 60,000 and 90,000 words to play with, this will give you ample room to explore your characters, their motivations, and the situation in which they find themselves.

First things count

The first few pages of a novel are the most important. They will make the reader decide whether it's worth reading on. So you need to grab his or her attention, for example by starting in the middle of a conversation or with a striking event. Look at the first pages of top-selling novels and you'll find that they nearly always begin with a striking event or conversation.

PLANNING, PLANNING AND MORE PLANNING

As with a mainstream novel, the erotic novel needs an underlying plot: that is, **character** and **conflict** and **conclusion**. So where does your plot start? And should your book/story start with the plot, the character, or the setting?

Plot or character first?

Writers in the genre are divided as to whether the plot or the character comes first. Cleo Cordell starts her books with a character and setting – although she admits that the emphasis is mostly on the setting: 'Something with lots of sensual possibilities, somewhere interesting that I'll enjoy writing about.' Zak Jane Keir uses a wide variety of starting points, from a name, a place, a storyline or even a theory. Best-selling writer Portia da Costa usually starts with the idea of the book; Mary Tofts' work usually revolves around a strong group of characters; and Eliza Down's first novel was sparked off by a scenario which turned into a plot. Whatever inspires you – use it.

Developing a plot

One good way to develop a plot is to start with the idea, then ask 'what if . . . ?' Keep asking the question, and your plot will start to take shape.

Some people find plotting easy; others, such as Portia da Costa, find it the hardest thing. 'I spend long hours just trying to work it out beforehand, weighing up causes and effects and twists *etc*, but usually find that once I get working, plot points seem to suggest themselves. It is a huge struggle, though.'

Mary Tofts adds, 'If I'd had a quid for every ending I've agonised over . . . the only way round it is to edit and re-edit and play with different ideas – you'll know when you've hit on the right one. It took me ages to get the ending of my story *Neil You Horror!* right, the breakthrough coming when I decided what the ring which Neil had made for his heroine would look like – it was all relatively straightforward after that.'

Using a flow diagram

One way to help you sketch out your plot is to do a **flow diagram** – using a bare bones approach – and see where it leads you. See Figure 2 on page 40 for an example of the beginning of a plot and the kinds of questions you can ask to help develop the plot.

Structuring your flow chart

Start with your basic idea and draw a box round it. For example, supposing that your main character is a woman who has buried herself in work. Something happens – either she has a huge row with her boss, or she's made redundant, or her company is taken over and she has a clash with her new boss. Her friends suggest that she takes a break and she agrees, reluctantly, to do so. What happens next – does she meet someone on her journey? What happens when she reaches her destination? Does it have anything to do with her encounter on her journey? Do her feelings towards her boss affect the choices she makes?

Box each event, then draw a line between each consecutive event. Don't forget to link back to 'connecting' events – for example, in the plot outlined above, if the woman encounters someone on her journey and then again when she reaches her destination, there will be a line linking that event with her arrival (the next part of the story) and also with what happens next. If your plot is completely linear, there will be no links back to events that

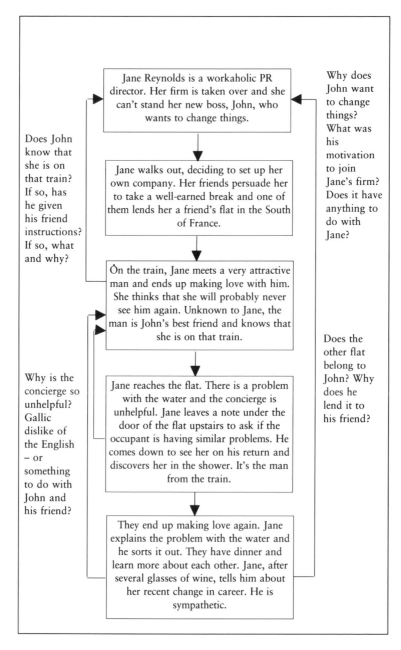

Fig. 2. Example beginning of a flow chart.

happened earlier in the story, and your reader will find the plot too simple.

Seeing plot complexities at a glance

Using a flow diagram means that you can see at a glance where there will be room for extra 'branches' (or sub-plots). If your flow diagram resembles a spider's web, it's possible that your plot has become too complex; you can see immediately where the likely areas of confusion will be, and deal with them accordingly.

Once your basic plot is sketched out, you can then break it down into chapters, and put flesh on the bones. Now that you have the characters, the basic outline of the plot, and the setting, you're ready to work on your novel. This means planning, planning and more planning – and the best way to do this is to write a synopsis.

WRITING A SYNOPSIS

If you used a flow-chart diagram for your plot, use it to build your synopsis. This will help to give you a working structure, when you're writing the novel. Try to divide the book into a sensible number of chapters, for example 12 chapters for a 60,000-word book and 16 chapters for an 80,000-word book. The chapters don't all have to be exactly the same length – but if they're approximately the same length, that is, somewhere between 4500 and 5500 words, the book will seem more balanced.

The different types of synopsis

Working synopsis
You need two different types of synopsis, to do two different jobs. The first is your 'working' synopsis. This is the synopsis you will work from when you write your novel: that is, a detailed break-down of the book's characters, setting and action, split into chapters.

Selling synopsis
The second type of synopsis is a much shorter version of your working synopsis. This is your 'selling' synopsis, which you will send to editors as part of your submission, whether you're sending just the first three chapters or the whole novel.

Structuring your synopsis

For your working synopsis, the first paragraph of your synopsis should introduce your main characters, the setting, and what is happening. Then you should work through the plot, chapter by chapter, showing what happens and where characters develop.

Use the amount of detail that suits you best

If you prefer to work from a very detailed plan, then put in as much detail as you like; if you know from previous experience that you tend to change things as you go along, then put in less detail – just enough to help you remember what you want to do with the plot.

For your 'selling' synopsis, remember that most editors prefer to read no more than three A4 pages, typed in double-spacing. The first paragraph of this synopsis should give a brief overview of the novel: this should take no more than six lines. What you're trying to do is to rouse the editor's interest – just as the blurb on the back of a book jacket and the extract from the novel on the prelim page tries to rouse the reader's interest.

Then give a very brief resume of your main characters – their names, ages, occupations and a brief description of their looks will do – and state whether your setting is contemporary or historical (if the latter, name the period), where it is, and whether it's fictional or real. Finally, outline each chapter, giving roughly six to ten lines for each chapter.

See Figure 3 on page 43 for the first page of an example selling synopsis – for *Dangerous Consequences* by Pamela Rochford, published by Black Lace.

WORKING TO A SYNOPSIS

If you're writing your book before submitting it to an editor, don't feel that you have to stick rigidly to the synopsis. Go with your instinct. If you get a better idea for an ending when you're halfway through the book, or an event happens partway through your book and changes the plot, use it. The same goes for characters. If a new character writes himself or herself into the book, it's usually for the better.

If you're selling your book on the basis of a synopsis and the first three chapters, you have rather less room for manoeuvre. Most professional writers allow themselves to deviate from their

Dangerous consequences
– a contemporary erotic novel by Pamela Rochford

After an erotically-charged conflict with an influential man at the university, Rachel is under threat of redundancy. Luke takes her to a friend's for a weekend in the country, to cheer her up. When she returns to London, she's accused of smuggling papers out of the country, and sacked on the spot. In the meantime, Luke has disappeared. What is the link between Luke, Max, his friends and the missing papers? Is Luke really what he seems? Was the erotic charge between them just to throw her off the scent and disguise what they were really doing?

Main characters
Rachel Kemp is 30; she's a junior lecturer in English at a London university. She's writing a thesis on the role of women in the Victorian novel, as part of her doctorate, although she's finding it difficult – she clashes badly with Colin Gilson, her head of department, who's supervising her thesis. She's 5 foot 3, with blonde curly hair, hazel eyes and a lush figure; she tends to dress in leggings and loose sweaters (chiffon loose shirts, if she has to dress up). She lives alone, in Walthamstow.

Luke Holloway is 27; he's a lecturer in economic history who has spent the past three years working in America. He lives in Holborn, in a rented flat. He's tall, with dark hair and greeny-grey eyes; he's nice-looking, and tends to wear faded jeans and baggy sweaters outside university.

The setting
London; a fictional country house in Norfolk.

The plot
Rachel is working in the library on a Saturday morning. On her way back from the coffee machine, she's not looking where she's going and collides with a man. Her coffee ruins his paperwork; Luke says that she can start apologising by taking him for a coffee.

Over coffee, they tell each other more about themselves. Rachel explains about her problems; he says that she needs something to take her mind off it – he doesn't have any answers, but says that dinner would be a start. Rachel agrees, and spends the afternoon fantasising about him. Over dinner, she finds herself growing more and more turned on by him.

Fig. 3. Example synopsis first page.

synopsis, but do check with your publisher before you make any radical alterations.

USING COMMON PLOTS TO THEIR BEST ADVANTAGE

It's said that in fiction, there are only seven basic plots, based on the seven deadly sins. If we take that view to the obvious conclusion, erotic fiction only has one – lust! However, even the most skilled writer couldn't rehash the same plot for dozens and dozens of books. It would be too predictable, and the audience would grow bored.

The list of common plots below could be expanded quite easily, but these are the main ones used by top-selling writers.

Initiation

This isn't just the standard 'how Jane lost her virginity' story, and it doesn't necessarily have to be an older man introducing a younger woman to sex. The initiation story can also show a character's exploration of different sorts of sexuality. Particularly popular are:

● Initiation into darker sexuality – usually involving corporal punishment, with the emphasis on shame rather than pain; corporal punishment and SM themes are a very popular sub-genre within erotica.

● Initiation into a secret society or club, whose members explore their sexuality and recognise each other by some kind of insignia – Cyrian Amberlake's *The Domino Tattoo* has inspired several contemporary novels on this theme.

Make sure that you don't position the book as an autobiography, though. Erotic autobiographies can be an incredibly tedious read (for example, the Victorian *Walter* books), and it's not appropriate to the erotic novel.

The job which leads to an erotic situation

Accepting a job (or meeting a new boss) which leads to an erotic situation is another popular plot – although be warned, there are a plethora of novels about wealthy barons and housekeepers around, and editors are becoming bored with them. This can be combined with the 'initiation' theme, for example with a teacher seducing his or her pupil. (Note that the pupil will be over the age of consent.)

The house which takes over people's lives
The setting is the most important part of this type of plot; the house can be inherited or bought, but the important thing is that the main character's life/sexuality is changed by the move.

The episodic tale
A novel where each chapter tells a different story which is linked to the preceding and following chapters. This is along the same kind of lines as the *Arabian Nights* or *Scheherezade*, with the hero or heroine embarking on a series of sexual adventures. The link between the stories needs to be very tight, though, or your book will look like a cobbled-together batch of stories or just a string of sex-scenes, which will bore the reader.

Power games
Editor Kerri Sharp says that novels featuring power games or power relationships are among the most popular with Black Lace readers, with characters who, sexually, 'surrender responsibility to someone else. They want exciting and experimental sex, but they don't want to be ashamed by having to ask for it . . . Our readers like to read about men who take the initiative sexually and are confident.'

Conflict
Conflict between your characters is a very good way of helping the plot move forward. Some of the most likely causes of conflict (which have a lot in common with romance) are:

- family feuds
- cultural/political differences
- money/class
- jobs
- lifestyle clash.

AVOIDING OVERUSED DEVICES

Overused plots
Certain plots have, as Kerri Sharp states in the Black Lace guidelines, been done to death. These include:

- women's health clubs 'with a difference'
- contact magazines
- sex as therapy
- impossibly wealthy suitors
- the sex industry.

Overused situations
Also avoid using clichéd situations; Elizabeth Coldwell, editor of *Forum*, says, 'There are far too many stories about neighbours popping round for sugar and having sex instead.'

Taboo areas
The final kind of plots and plot elements to avoid are the taboo areas. These are non-consensual sex and anything illegal, such as:

- Incest. Even if you think you're being very clever by using the Oedipus myth, it won't get past your editor.

- Under-age sex. The Victorian 'cult of the little girl' does not exist in our age. Make sure that all your characters – heterosexual or homosexual – are above the age of consent, if they're going to have sex. If you're using a historical setting which had a different age of consent, make sure that you get the details right.

- Bestiality.

If you include any of the above, you'll either have an immediate rejection letter or, if it's only part of the book, you'll be asked to rewrite it, removing the unacceptable elements. Even the 'initiation into the world of SM' type books steer clear of non-consensual sex.

Also note that some editors are not keen on male homosexual scenes, particularly if the imprint is aimed mainly at a male readership.

UNDERSTANDING THE ROLE OF 'SET PIECES'

A common remark about erotic novels is that they're filled with
set pieces, or scenes which appear in many novels. Remember that
any sexual action needs to further the plot – if it's there just for
the sake of padding the word-count, it will show.

Making the most of the 'set piece'

Variety
Try to vary the sexual action. As Kerri Sharp says, 'It's possible
to write an arousing story where characters only have beautiful
and meaningful sex in bed, naked, under the duvet, but it's pretty
boring when you have an entire gamut of sexual behaviour to play
with.'

Is it physically possible?
Make sure that whatever action you describe is physically possible.
For example, if your characters have sex standing up, it depends
on their height as to whether it's comfortable; and if the woman
is lifted against the wall, she won't be 5 foot 10 and weigh 20
stone, while her partner is 5 foot 6 and weighs ten stone.

Common set pieces which many top writers use include:

- the scene set in a bath or shower

- the outdoor romp

- the lesbian or homosexual fantasy (note that the latter isn't
  popular in books aimed at a male or a mixed audience)

- the threesome fantasy or orgy

- the masturbation scene (sometimes linked with telephone
  sex; also commonly linked with email or computer tech-
  nology)

- the corporal punishment scene (whips, chains, canes, slippers,
  hairbrushes and the like)

- the bondage or blindfold scene

- voyeurism (often involving two-way mirror or being hidden
  in a wardrobe, roof or the next room with a peep-hole)

- the 'foodie' scene – with a character using whipped cream, honey and champagne *etc* on his or her lover's body

- the erotic massage.

These scenes can be very effective, or they can be extremely hackneyed – it's up to you, the writer, to make sure that it's the former. If it doesn't do anything for you, it will show in your writing: so only write what you enjoy.

Asking for comments
Once you've written the scene, ask your 'audience of one' to read it and comment; for example, if the response is a groan of, 'Oh, not, not *that* again,' or laughter, you need to rewrite or even scrap the scene.
See Chapter 6 for advice on writing the sex scene.

CHECKLIST

From your flow chart and working synopsis, check whether your plot is complex enough to interest the reader – but not so complex that the reader is confused as to what is going on.

- Look at your 'selling' synopsis and check that it reflects your book accurately, giving the editor a 'hook' to sell the book to readers.

- Make sure that you avoid the overused plot and situation elements.

- Make sure that you avoid plot and situation elements that the editor will find unacceptable.

CASE STUDIES

Edward loses direction
Edward is an English student who wants to supplement his grant by writing novels. He knows that the erotic market is one of the easier markets to break into, and has researched the market thoroughly. He knows which publisher he wants to target and which are the favourite themes of his chosen imprint, and he has

read the guidelines thoroughly. However, he doesn't plan his novel, trusting that the action will resolve itself through the interaction of his characters – and he runs out of steam halfway through the book.

Felicity swerves from her structure

Felicity is a saleswoman who finds that her job really helps her to identify different types of character. Her love of reading inspires her to unlimited plots, and she always write a full synopsis before she starts work on a novel. However, she finds that the interaction between her characters makes her deviate from her synopsis to such an extent that the finished book is nothing like her original idea. To give her the best chance of selling her books, Felicity always writes the book first and then revamps her synopsis to suit before submitting her manuscript to an editor.

ASSIGNMENT

Start from a basic premise of the story of Snow White and see how many different plots you can get out of it (with a chain of 'what ifs').

4
Developing Your Characters

CREATING YOUR CHARACTERS

Identifying with your characters

Character is as important in the erotic novel as in any other type of fiction. You need to identify with your main character, and find his or her lover sexy – if you don't, how can you expect your readers to believe in your characters and sympathise with them? For that reason, many successful writers use themselves – or part of themselves – in their characters, with a bit of fantasy thrown in.

Using your own characteristics for your lead character
For example, if you're a female writer, your female lead character might have the attributes you like in yourself, plus the attributes you'd like to have. For example, she might have your hair colour and style, but be taller or thinner. She might be able to speak seven languages, or fix cars, or paint, or program computers. She might look like Meg Ryan or Julie Christie or Vivien Leigh. If you're a male writer, your male lead character might have the, same occupation and hobbies as you, but have different colour eyes, be able to play the piano, or look like David Duchovny or James Dean. Or he might race cars for a living. If that's what you would really like to do, your passion for the subject will come across in your book, and give your novel more impact.

Mixing fact and fantasy

The lead character of the opposite sex can also be a mixture of **fact** and **fantasy**. He or she might look like a famous actor or sportsperson or singer. He or she might have your own lover's eye colour. He could be anything from a James Bond or Indiana Jones swashbuckling type to the 'quiet but deep' man you've noticed in a corner of the office and wondered what he was really like; and she could be anything from a cool and sexy Dana Scully to a bright and bubbly Anthea Turner type. The important thing is that you find him or her attractive, because your attitude to your character will certainly affect your readers' view of your character.

Looking at viewpoint and interaction

The **viewpoint** in your novel or story will probably be from a character's who is the same sex as you are – mainly because it's very difficult to sustain a novel written from the opposite sex's viewpoint and keep it plausible. So imagine that you are the character you've just invented. If you looked like him or her, thought like him or her, had his or her quick temper or assertiveness or talent, how would you react in the situations demanded by your plot? How would you react to the other characters – as a friend, a lover, an enemy or a colleague?

Using only one viewpoint per scene
When you're writing the novel, you need to stick to the viewpoint of one character in each scene, or your readers will become confused. This is particularly true of 'flashback' scenes. If you're recounting an event in the past as seen by Adam, suddenly switching into Becky's view of the scene throws the reader off balance. There are better ways to write in an element of surprise.

The **interaction** between your characters is what will really interest your readers. How do your characters interact? If one is submissive and one is dominant, who is really the one who controls the action? Remember, it isn't necessarily the outwardly dominant one.

Considering the number of characters

It's possible to write a book using just two characters – but it might be too intense or too boring for your readers. You need other characters, if only to throw your main characters into relief. Even in an 'enclosed' setting, such as among the clientèle of an exclusive hotel, you need to have interaction between various characters.

Using lots of characters
Editors like to have varied scenes, not just a long saga of Anna and Bryan's lovemaking alone in the novel. What about Charles and David and Elizabeth, and the permutations? Anna and Bryan,

Anna and Charles, Anna and David, Anna and Elizabeth, Anna and Bryan and Charles . . . Though make sure that you're not throwing in the sex scenes just to pad out the novel. If Anna and Bryan are an established couple, Anna needs to have some kind of motivation to make love with Charles or David or Elizabeth – motivation which furthers the plot.

Avoiding overpopulation
On the other hand, if you populate your novel with as many people as Dickens did, you're at risk of your characters becoming ciphers for the sexual action – particularly as an erotic novel is a great deal shorter than the average Dickens novel – and your readers will find this unsatisfying because the plot of your novel will be submerged under the weight of the huge cast of characters. Go for the happy medium.

Making sure that your characters are consistent

You need to keep a note of certain things about your characters – such as eye colour – for continuity's sake. It can be argued that it's the job of a copy-editor to pick up that your lead female character has blue eyes in chapter one, but has brown eyes in chapter eleven when you changed your mind and forgot to alter the references in chapter one – but copy-editors are not infallible. If your work is sloppy, there's always a chance that something will be missed. Don't cheat your readers by skimping your checks on the details.

Your characters also need to be consistent in their behaviour. Of course, everyone has mood-swings; but a character who's assertive one minute, passive the next, and then assertive again will simply confuse your readers (unless it's obvious sexual role-play, but then it's likely to involve one of the specialist sorts of fiction).

Using a potted biography

One way to help keep your characters consistent is to use a **potted biography** or a thumbnail sketch, and refer back to it while you're writing. It's particularly useful if you have a character in chapter one who doesn't appear again until halfway through the book: by then, you'll be so involved in your other characters that you'll probably have forgotten the details of this character. Looking up his or her details in a 'potted biography' is much easier and quicker

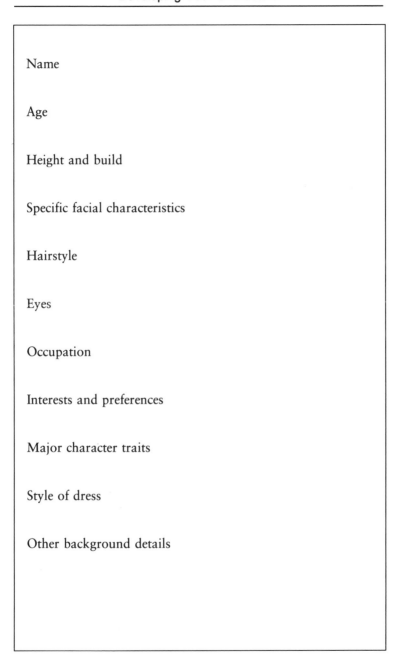

Name

Age

Height and build

Specific facial characteristics

Hairstyle

Eyes

Occupation

Interests and preferences

Major character traits

Style of dress

Other background details

Fig. 4. Sample form for a character's potted biography.

than having to re-read the whole of your first chapter to find out those same details.

Many successful writers prepare thumbnail sketches of their characters before they write the book. These don't have to be exhaustive. For example, Eliza Down and Zak Jane Keir both use very loose notes, and Cleo Cordell writes very brief notes, finding that her characters come to life as she writes about them.

Whether you use index cards, or just a piece of paper, try making a list of your main characters' attributes and refer back to it. Use a scaled-down version for your minor characters. An example form for a character's 'potted biography' is in Figure 4.

Looking at what readers want to know about your characters

There are a number of details about your characters that readers will want to know.

Age
How old is your character? This can be exact, for example 29, or approximate, for example mid-thirties. Star signs are probably not important, unless it's an intrinsic part of the plot.

Body type
What is the character's height and build? Is he or she tall or short, voluptuous, wiry or slender? But don't go into bra sizes – they really aren't necessary and can turn your description into farce or sleaze. Also avoid the 'busty blonde' syndrome – it's more of a caricature than anything else. At the same time, all your female characters don't all need to be tall and slender. Use a body type that you can identify with, either your own or what you would like to be, in an ideal world.

Facial characteristics
Does the character have any specific facial characteristics? For example, what is the character's facial shape – oval, square-jawed, heart-shaped? Does he or she have any scars or a broken nose or a beauty spot? Is he clean-shaven? Does she always wear make-up – and if so, what kind of colours does she use? If she usually sports the 'clean-scrubbed' look, what happens when she does use make-up?

Good-looking – or not?
Does the character have conventional good looks or is he or she unconventionally attractive? If you've borrowed the character's looks from a real person, you could write down their name in your notes as a reminder to you when you're writing – but be aware of the laws of libel. Don't say that your character *is* that real-life person, although you can say that your character reminds another of that real-life famous person.

Hairstyle
What sort of hairstyle does your character have? Think of the colour, the length, and whether it's straight or curly, natural or dyed. It's quite acceptable to have heroes who are thinning or bald – think how many women find Bruce Willis, André Agassi and Sean Connery attractive.

Eyes
What colour eyes does the character have? Do they change according to mood? If so, how? Does he or she wear glasses or contact lenses? If the former, what kind of style and frame? If the latter, are the lenses colour-enhanced? Does the character use coloured lenses as a disguise, for any reason?

Occupation
What does your character do for a living? You don't need to go into great depths about the character's career to date, unless it's an intrinsic part of the plot.

Interests and preferences
What are the character's interests and preferences? This is particularly important if the interests and preferences have a bearing on the plot, such as a love of Victorian paintings.

Personality traits
Does the character have any major personality traits? For example, is he or she shy, confident or arrogant? Is she a leader? Is he a follower? Do they discover different traits within themselves during the course of the novel – for example a woman who always thought of herself as a coward is put into a situation where she is forced to act bravely?

Dress
What is the character's favoured style of dress? Formal or casual,
scruffy or smart? This can also have a bearing on the plot – for
example, one of your female characters might believe herself only
to be attracted to professional men in dark suits and crisp white
shirts, but then meets a scruffy student who gives her a whole new
outlook on life. Also bear in mind the 'fetish value' of clothes,
particularly in historical novels.

Other background details
Are there any other background details that your readers should
know, because they have an impact on the plot? For example,
education or family circumstances.

Showing your characters to your readers
Having your characters looking at themselves in a mirror and
describing themselves is one way of telling your readers what the
characters look like – but be warned that some editors absolutely
hate that kind of scene. (See page 105 for comments from Mike
Bailey, editor of Headline Delta and Liaisons.)

The impact shocked him; he hadn't been aware that anyone else was
browsing in the same section of the library as he was. He turned to
stare at whoever had bumped into him, and caught his breath. She
was one of the most striking women he had ever seen. She wasn't
particularly tall – probably about five feet three – and she wasn't
particularly thin, but he was instantly attracted to her.

'Sorry,' she said, her voice low and cultured.

An intellectual, then. He would have known that even without the
tell-tale little round glasses which hid her cornflower blue eyes. She
looked a bit like a student, dressed in faded denims, a baggy sweater
and black leather ankle-boots. She wore no jewellery apart from a
watch with a leather strap and a large face. Her hair was light brown;
it was parted on one side and was slightly wavy, as if she were
growing out a perm.

Her skin was pale, as though she spent most of her time indoors.
Her mouth was wide and generous, with a full lower lip: a soft pale
rosy colour, a perfect cupid's bow that made him itch to draw his
tongue along it.

Fig. 5. An example of introducing a character.

An easier way is to describe the first time that one of your main character sees the other. For an example, see Figure 5.

A ROSE BY ANY OTHER NAME

Names are a small but important part of your character. It's unlikely that a Percy will be drop-dead sexy; nor will a Hilda (although a Hildebrand or Percival might be, if you're writing a book which has a medieval setting). On the other hand, your characters don't all have to have exotic names: one Angelica or Gabriella in a book is enough. It's perfectly all right to have a Jane and a Susan and a John and a Peter.

Often, you'll find that your characters will 'name' themselves. Though if a surname or first name is proving difficult, a quick trawl through the telephone directory or a book of babies' names will pay dividends.

UNDERSTANDING THE DIFFERENT TYPES OF EROTIC CHARACTERS

As with all genre fiction, the characters in erotic novels fall into **types**. This doesn't mean that your characters will be stereotypes – merely that they conform to certain conventions. If you're writing a 'power relationship' type novel, one of your lead characters will be dominant and the other will be submissive – but it's up to you which is which, and what other characteristics are blended with that particular one.

Looking at male character types

- '*Mr Rochester*' – he is sexually sophisticated, usually dominant, and usually well-educated. He's often rich (and can therefore afford to indulge his sexual fantasies whenever and however he likes); he's occasionally titled. Don't make him impossibly wealthy.

- *The naive man being taught new things* – his naïveté is his main characteristic, and it appeals to the female readers who would enjoy teaching a man what they know. He isn't stupid, or crass: he's usually young (although he's always over the age of consent).

- *The submissive man* – as a foil to a dominant female.

Looking at female character types

- *The naive woman being taught new things* – the female counterpart to the naive man, above.

- *The sophisticated woman with jaded appetites* – the female counterpart to 'Mr Rochester', above.

- *The independent free spirit.*

- *The successful businesswoman* who's thrown into the deep end or who has suppressed her sexuality and 'rediscovers' it.

- *The submissive woman*, as a foil to a dominant male.

USING DIALOGUE FOR A PURPOSE

The purpose of dialogue is to further the plot or to give your reader an insight into a character.

Throat-clearing
Avoid everyday conversations, and using lots of 'mm' and 'oh' and 'well' (referred to by editors as **throat-clearing,** and usually taken out at the copy-editing stage, because it's usually unnecessary padding).

Don't use dialogue to pad your story
Another form of unnecessary padding is to use the characters' names a lot, in dialogue. Avoid it. If your word-count is short, add another scene – don't go through and put the characters' names into every piece of dialogue, because it will be edited out. In real life, a conversation wouldn't run along the lines of:

'Hello, Jane. How are you?'
'Fine, thanks, Peter. How are you?'
'I'm very well, Jane. What are you doing, this evening?'
'Not much, Peter. What are you doing?'

So although the occasional reference to names is fine, don't do it in every speech.

The best way to check if your dialogue works is to read it aloud into a tape recorder, then play it back and listen hard. Or ask a friend to read it to you. Where are the weak points? Is all of it necessary? Where can you pare your dialogue to make it punchier and more immediate?

Being careful with accents

Not everyone speaks with a Home Counties BBC-newsreader accent. If you use a regional setting, the likelihood is that at least one character in your story will have a regional accent. That's fine – but don't try to convey it by using phonetic spellings, which will irritate your reader. 'Thass roit, gal,' may be exactly what an old Norfolk man would say, but write it as, 'That's right, girl.' 'Oi'm Oirish' is another one to avoid.

Using he said, she said

You don't always need to signpost who's talking for your readers. If it's already obvious that the dialogue is between two people, you don't have to keep writing 'Peter said' or 'Jane said' after each piece of dialogue. It's intrusive and looks more like you're trying to fill up the word-count (and editors are wise to this method of trying to pad out your novel). Though if it's a protracted piece of dialogue, using the occasional 'Peter said' and 'Jane said' will remind your readers who is speaking.

When describing tone, you don't always need to use adverbs. 'Peter said happily . . . Jane said crossly . . . Peter said pleadingly . . . Jane said intractably . . .' Using an adverb after every piece of speech soon makes your dialogue monotonous and irritates your reader. Use other verbs, instead, to convey tone. Whispered (though avoid 'whispered quietly' or 'shouted loudly' – these are obvious!), snapped, pleaded, cajoled, added . . . are all more evocative than 'said quietly', 'said crossly' *etc.*

CHECKLIST

Use this checklist to analyse a piece of your own writing.

- Make sure that your readers can *see* your characters – have you described them adequately? (Bear in mind that once you've 'set' the character, you don't have to keep repeating that he or she has blue eyes or dark hair or a Rubenesque figure.)

- Make sure that your characters are consistent and don't switch moods too often.

- Check that your dialogue has purpose and if it doesn't further the plot or characterisation, cut it.

- Make sure that you use verbs to convey tone, rather than adverbs. Remember, less is more.

CASE STUDIES

Gary works on his dialogue
Gary finds writing dialogue difficult. He knows that he has a bad habit of making his characters say 'oh' and 'um', not furthering the plot or the reader's knowledge of the character. To help himself improve, he reads his dialogue into a tape-recorder and plays it back, listening critically and thinking about what he's heard. Then he edits his manuscript, taking out the redundant words and conversational trivia. He checks his dialogue again with the help of the tape-recorder, and keeps editing until he feels that his dialogue is tight enough.

Helen has trouble with characters
Helen finds writing dialogue easy, and has structured her plots so that her book is well-paced. However, she knows her characters so well that she forgets to describe them, and when she submits her first manuscript, the editor rejects it because her characters aren't defined enough for her readers.

ASSIGNMENT

To help you practise characterisation, write thumbnail sketches of people you know – family, friends, colleagues; or even what you imagine a famous person to be like.

- What do they look like?
- What are their distinguishing features?

● What are their interests?

● How has their background influenced them?

Don't forget to include:

● mannerisms

● speech patterns and accents *etc*

● the way they walk.

5
Developing Your Setting

LOOKING AT HOW SETTINGS WORK

What is a setting?

Your setting is basically **where** the action in your book takes place, **when**, and the **world** in which your characters move. It could be anything from seventeenth-century Spain, to Roman Britain or present-day London. It could be a real-life location, or a fictional one that is based on somewhere you know. It could be set in the world of antiques or stockbroking or horse-riding.

Making it special

Whatever you use as your setting, you need to make it special by the way you describe it – particularly if you do know the setting well, because it's very easy to take it for granted and forget to describe it. It's important that your reader can *see* your setting. In the same way that your readers can only visualise your characters if you describe them, your readers can only see your settings if you describe them.

See Figure 6 for an example of scene-setting.

Creating the right atmosphere

Sexy places

Your setting needs to create the right atmosphere. Erotic novels need erotic settings – or settings which lend themselves to the erotic. To take an extreme example, an abattoir is hardly likely to turn your readers on – but a ruined abbey, a luxury apartment or a beach on the Whitsunday Islands with sand like white talcum powder might be the stuff of their own personal fantasies, and they'll really enjoy a book with that kind of setting. Think of the

It was the first time that she'd ever set foot in an artist's studio, and it was nothing like she had expected. For a start, it was incredibly neat and tidy; she'd expected tubes of paint to be lying around everywhere, and screwed-up paper from sketches which hadn't met his high standards.

It was an attic room in the terraced house, with windows on both sides – probably to catch the most light, she thought. She remembered hearing somewhere that artists liked north light, for some reason.

The sloping windows had no curtains, not even muslin nets, and the scrubbed and unpolished floorboards were bare, apart from a large rug in the middle of the floor. The design was obviously from the middle East somewhere – Dubai, perhaps, or Egypt – and it was probably silk, judging by the way that the colours changed in the light as she walked across the room.

There was a large table by one of the windows, with a drawing-board and various tools of the kind she'd seen in the window of a graphic art supplier's; there was also an easel, to the side, and a stack of canvases facing the wall. The whole place smelled vaguely of linseed oil: a scent which she'd never found particularly arousing before, but now made a tingle of excitement run through her. Would he oil her body with linseed oil, before he painted her? And then, after he'd drawn her, caught her form on canvas . . . The possibilities made her pulse beat faster.

Fig. 6. An example of scene-setting.

types of places that you think are sexy, and build on those kinds of scenario for your novel.

Sexy behaviour in unorthodox places

Inappropriate behaviour in a given setting can also be erotic. This is where workplace scenes can be very effective – for example, you could have a scene set in an office, with one of your female characters not wearing any underwear; or perhaps a character is working from home in a telesales role, and his or her lover tries to distract him or her in an erotic way, in the middle of the phone call. Or maybe you could have a character lewdly dressed in a snooty and upmarket surrounding; this is common in the 'power games' type novel – it is the inappropriateness that is arousing for your readers.

The effects of time
What kind of timescale should your novel span? It depends on your plot but, as mentioned in a previous chapter, long timescales such as those needed for an autobiography or a saga spanning four generations are not appropriate to the erotic novel. Usually, the timescale will be less than a year.

More than an historical period
Don't forget that time is more than just an historical period. At what time of year is your book set? What time of day do the scenes take place? This will affect your plot. For example, if your book is set in the South of France in August, it's unlikely that you'll have an outdoor sex-scene set in the middle of the day. It would be too hot and sticky; and even night-time would need careful handling, because of mosquitoes and gnats and midges. Similarly, if your book is set in the Lake District in January, you wouldn't have an outdoor sex-scene at all – it would be too cold.

Light and temperature
The time of day also affects light and temperature. In erotic writing, sensual descriptions are paramount; the different kinds of lighting (for example twilight, midday, dawn) will have an effect on your characters and their feelings, and even on the way they look. Faces look different in bright sunshine and in twilight, and different again in a brightly lit room or a candlelit boudoir. Use the effects of light to create atmosphere.

The same goes for temperature – your setting could be a warm and cosy indoor situation, contrasting with deep snow outside in winter; or cool and sensual in an orchard at daybreak on a summer morning. What kind of surroundings would make you feel sexy – a deserted beach, a castle, a hayfield, a fleecy rug in front of a roaring log fire, a conservatory filled with lush plants, a four-poster bed in a stately home? The type of surroundings that affect you will be the best surroundings to affect your characters, because the way you write about it will be more personal and more immediate.

Scent
Scent also has a part to play in building atmosphere. For example, if you have a scene where one of your characters is giving another character a massage, what kind of oils are being used? What do they smell like? What effect do those scents have on your

characters? Do any of your characters have a fetish about scent, for example vanilla or citrus?

Different places also have different smells, which may change with the season. Eucalyptus brings to mind a winter setting. Lavender, roses and honeysuckle equate to summer. The smell of bonfires is evocative of November, and the scent of fireworks that lingers for days afterwards. A country setting will maybe bring to mind apple blossom in spring and hayfields and the heavy pollen of an oilseed rape crop in summer; a seaside setting will have the freshness of ozone and the tang of salt in the air, whatever the season; and settings abroad will have their own particular scents, too.

Think about how those different scents make your characters act, and the kinds of feelings and thoughts they evoke.

Sound

If any of your characters indulge in blindfold-type games, scent and sound will often take the place of sight, so that your blindfolded character can make sense of his or her surroundings.

Sound is also another way of establishing a setting. What kind of music do your characters listen to, if anything? What kind of sounds are in their environment? Again, a novel set near the sea will have a different 'soundtrack' to one set in a country house or in the city – the sound of the ocean and seagulls rather than larks and woodpigeons or the bustle of traffic.

The effects of sound

Do any particular sounds have an erotic effect on your characters? For example, the wailing sound of Egyptian or Moroccan music might bring to mind a fantasy based around Middle Eastern dance for one character; another might find certain piano music arousing, making them fantasise about being Beethoven's or Mozart's lover; and another might think of an erotic scenario whenever he or she hears the sound of a waterfall.

If you decide to use music to 'soundtrack' your book, try to keep it as vague as possible. Remember that your reader might not necessarily share your musical tastes. It's probably better to talk about soft bluesy-rock or Mozart string quartets than to specify actual tracks by rock bands or movements in classical pieces, unless the music has a particular bearing on the plot.

Fitting your characters

Your setting needs to 'fit' your characters. You're very unlikely to have sophisticated jet-setters living in a little rural village (unless, of course, one of them owns a very large and sumptuous country house, and part of the action takes place there between some of the guests or the inhabitants). A lecturer or music teacher won't live alone in a sumptuous house in Hampstead (unless he or she inherited either the house or a large amount of money); someone who's made a fortune from software or stockbroking won't live in a cramped flat in one of the less salubrious districts of London. Be realistic – though not *too* realistic. Your readers want to fantasise, and poky bedsits don't have the same erotic potential as a light and airy house filled with plush soft furnishings and silk rugs.

Using what you know

Interests and hobbies

If you have a particular interest or hobby, think about using it as part of your setting. For example, if you play the cello, your novel could be set round an orchestra or a string quartet, or even include scenes between a music teacher and a pupil, with the pupil learning the arts of love as well as the arts of music. Because you know the world of music, your setting will be much more vivid and your readers will be able to identify more closely with it. Or maybe you've taken classes in Egyptian dancing or the lambada – the erotic potential of dance will work well in a novel.

Your occupation

Your occupation might inspire you – for example, if you work in advertising, or you're a picture restorer, or you're a landscape gardener, consider setting your novel in that kind of environment. Almost any job has some erotic potential, if you think about it. And because you know that environment well, you'll be able to describe it more vividly than an environment with which you're less familiar.

Local industry and tourist attractions

Your local industry, too, can be used for a successful setting. For example, if you live near a racecourse, you might be able to use that kind of environment as the setting for a scene. Or maybe you live near an iron-age fort – think of the exhilaration of walking its boundaries on a windy dawn in a large unbuttoned overcoat, feeling almost as if you could fly as the wind blows your coat wide open, then moving down into the sheltered part in the centre. How would your characters react in that setting? Would they find the sheer power of the wind an erotic spur?

The possibilities are endless. Imagine a couple boating on a lake – your characters could be making love in public but trying to give the appearance of nothing untoward happening. The physical constrictions of the boat and trying to remain almost fully clothed for propriety's sake can make for a very steamy encounter.

Watchpoints for your settings
Write about what you know, but be careful to avoid:

- *technical terms* – it's likely that your readers won't understand them, and explaining them will slow down the action and break the erotic mood

- *using real names of people or firms* – this is potentially libellous and will cause you all sorts of problems.

Recognising what works and what doesn't
Erotica is very intense, so it works very well in an 'enclosed' type setting, where real life can be left behind – though steer clear of harems. They've been done to death. The same is true of novels about decadent barons and their housekeepers in Hampstead.

Editors have mixed views about using the provinces and the metropolis. Small town locations are not popular with Black Lace, for example. If you do decide to use a provincial setting, make the most of it: 'passion in the shadow of the gasworks' isn't likely to appeal to your readers. If in doubt, stick to London, Paris, New York and the like.

Making background notes
These will be useful when you come to write your synopsis, and also when you're describing the setting in your novel. For example:

Historical or contemporary setting
Is your setting historical or contemporary? If it's an historical

novel, which period are you using – for example, Victorian, Elizabethan, Roman, or Georgian?

The country and local area
In which country does the action take place – and in which particular part? For example, you could set your book in the Cotswolds, Cornwall, or Brittany. You don't necessarily have to know the place well – research it, or use a fictional setting based on an actual part of the country.

Seasonal implications
What is the season/time of year, and how does the weather affect your setting?

Where your characters live
Where do your characters live? For example, in a castle, a stately home, a boat, a caravan or an old cottage? Remember the geography of rooms as well as the location; your readers will need to 'see' a room. For example, if one of your characters is an artist and you have an erotic scene evolving from a portrait sitting, what does his or her studio look like? Colours, textures, materials, lighting – these are all important, to help fix the scene in your reader's mind.

Minor characters who live with your main characters
Who lives with your characters? It's fine to include cats or dogs here, as signposts to your readers about your characters' personality: but don't give the animals more than a 'walk-on' part, and keep them out of the sex scenes. It's probably not a good idea to have characters living at home with their parents or grandparents – unless, perhaps, you're writing a power games novel and your character is a decoy who leads the hero/heroine to the real 'master' – who just happens to be that character's parent.

Transport
How do your characters move about in your setting? For example, do they walk, drive, ride on horseback, use a boat or public transport? If you use London as a setting, make sure you know which tube stops the characters use – don't put Hampstead on the Central line or Oxford Street on the East London line.

Real or fictional setting
Is the setting a 'real' place or a fictional one? If it's the former, make sure that your topographical and geographical details are correct; if it's the latter, be careful not to use the name of a real place.

USING POPULAR SETTINGS

Some settings are very popular with readers. These include:

● historical (particularly for women's fiction – and there are thousands of years to choose from, so don't limit yourself to Paris in the 1920s)

● the country house or castle

● an exclusive hotel

● the office or place of work (which could be anything from a library to a laboratory to a high-tech office).

WHICH SETTINGS TO AVOID

Certain settings have been done to death in the erotic novel, and editors would prefer you to avoid them. These include:

● health clubs 'with a difference'
● luxury yachts
● harems
● nightclubs
● Paris in the 1920s
● Edwardian England
● the Victorian era
● the sex industry.

Some settings are unpopular with readers, and therefore are not popular with editors. These include:

● futuristic/science fiction backgrounds
● fantasy fiction (mythical creatures, magic and the like)
● the paranormal (even for X-philes!).

The major imprints prefer contemporary erotic novels, though historical settings are popular in women's erotica.

UNDERSTANDING THE IMPORTANCE OF RESEARCH

If you decide to use an exotic location, particularly one where you haven't stayed for a long enough period to know it really well, make sure that you research it properly. Check that any flowers or trees or animals you describe really do have their habitat in your setting. Are you really likely to find orchids growing wild in Rhodes, or tigers in Africa, or kangaroos in Arizona?

Sadly, it's unlikely that the taxman will accept a luxury four-week trip to the Seychelles as a legitimate business expense – but the local library may have some good information about your chosen setting, or you may have friends who have visited the place and can give you some idea of the atmosphere. You could also try writing off to tourist offices or hotels or travel agents for brochures and recommendations for other media – for example, a promotional video about your proposed setting might be available.

Finding out what you don't know

If you're setting the novel in part of Britain you haven't visited, and don't have friends who can tell you what the area is like, use an ordnance survey map to make sure that you have the geographical details as accurate as possible. For example, there are no caves in Norfolk (as one editor had to tell an author!). If you refer to train stations, airports or ports, make sure that they exist. Check your road names – the M1 does not go through Suffolk, and the A47 is not in Cornwall.

Having said that, it's perfectly acceptable to use a fictional setting. Avoid using a real place name if you use a fictional setting. It's easy to make up a place name – simply chop two place names in half, and then join them up to the other halves. For example, Lucinda Chester's novel *Spring Fever* is set in a fictional Norfolk village called Happisthorpe; the village name was created by using this method and borrowing the first parts of the place names Thorpe St Andrew and Happisburgh.

Historical settings

Historical settings need even more care than contemporary settings. Research the clothes, the food, and the social history – there are plenty of good books which cover social life in various historical eras. Don't let anachronisms creep in, such as medieval maidens wearing nylon stockings, Elizabethan Cavaliers, or fourteenth-century monks wearing watches. If you mention food, make sure that it had been imported to your chosen setting at that point in time – for example, don't talk about potatoes or chocolate in Roman Britain.

CHECKLIST

● Make sure that you know your setting well (either through experience or research) – it's likely that some of your readers will also know that world well, and inconsistencies and misconceptions will irritate them.

● Avoid settings which have been 'done to death' – unless you can think of a really original twist.

● Make sure that your timescale is consistent – for example, don't jump from spring to winter and back to spring again in the space of a couple of chapters (excluding flashbacks).

● Read through your manuscript again. Are you sure that a reader who doesn't know your setting can 'see' it?

CASE STUDIES

Isabel researches the Greek islands
Isabel's novel is contemporary, partly set on an archaeological dig in Samos, a Greek island just off Turkey. She has never visited Samos but has researched her setting thoroughly by borrowing books from the library, visiting travel agents to collect brochures, and writing away to the tourist office for more information. She now feels confident that she knows the island well enough to set her story there.

Julian sits on the fence
Julian took up fencing a couple of years ago and enjoys his twice-weekly bout. He writes an historical erotic novel based in the seventeenth century, and uses his knowledge of fencing to great

effect in a scene about a duel, bringing the book to life. He's careful not to use technical terms, sticking to the descriptions of the various movements rather than their names, as he knows that not all his readers will know the difference between a lunge and a riposte.

ASSIGNMENT

Look out of the window and write down exactly what you see. Try it in various locations. Then read what you've written to someone else who knows the place you've written about – can they guess what you're describing? Do they think that you've missed anything? If you have, can you justify leaving it out? If not, it will probably show you where your weak spots are likely to be when describing the setting in your novel.

6
Writing the Sex Scene

THE ROLE OF SEX IN THE EROTIC NOVEL

The whole point of the erotic novel or story is to be a good read which also arouses the reader through scenes of explicit sexual action.

Your editor will expect around 50 per cent of the action in your erotic novel to be sexually explicit, and for the first sex scene to start within the first ten or so pages of the novel – certainly by the end of the first chapter, at the very latest. That isn't to say that you can't have a plot: just that the plot has to be inextricably linked to an erotic theme.

Figure 7 is an example of the beginning of a sex scene.

MAKING A START

A lot of writers have problems with their first sex scene. It's embarrassing, writing a sex scene – it's like being a voyeur. And even worse, you're encouraging your readers to be voyeurs, too! Before you start writing, you need to lose any inhibitions you have about writing sex scenes, or you'll find that the uphill struggle becomes too steep and you either leave the scene unfinished, or your writing is unsuccessful.

Writing about what you enjoy

Take a step back and think logically. You're writing an erotic scene. If it's going to fulfil its purpose in the book and turn your readers on, it's likely to turn you on, too. Erotic writer Alan York speaks for many successful authors of erotica when he says, 'My libido is my first and best critic.' So write about something that you enjoy, something that gives you the '*mm*' factor when you're reading it over.

He bent his head and kissed her, his lips sensual and persuasive as they moved against hers. Sally couldn't help responding, twining her hands round his neck and opening her mouth, letting his tongue explore her.

When he broke the kiss, she was shaking. He stroked her face. 'Okay?' he asked softly.

She nodded, not trusting herself to speak. God, there really was something about him – something that made her sex heat and her mind itch to do all sorts of wild and crazy things with him. With any of her past lovers, she would have been embarrassed if they'd kissed her passionately in the street like that – but with Robert, she'd wanted it to go further. She'd wanted him to touch her, slide his hands under her sweater and stroke the soft undersides of her breasts, play with her nipples, uncaring of who saw them and what they thought.

She shivered. If she wasn't careful, she could let herself go completely out of control.

Fig. 7. Example of the beginning of a sex scene.

Don't write about things that you don't enjoy

The reverse also holds true: if you don't feel comfortable reading or writing about certain sexual practices – for example, bondage or spanking and the kinds of corporal punishment found in an SM scene, or homosexual/lesbian sex – it will show in your manuscript, and your reader will feel distaste and disappointment when they read those scenes, rather than the enjoyment they expected to feel.

The important thing is to write about what you enjoy rather than what you think you *ought* to write about. A sex scene isn't sexy unless *you* feel that it's sexy. You don't have to have a whips-and-chains scene in every chapter, or even once in a book, if you don't want to. There's nothing wrong with 'vanilla' or gentle sex, if you describe it with enough feeling – though it's unlikely that you'll be targeting a publisher whose imprint deals with darker sex scenes and SM. There's also nothing wrong with writing an extremely kinky scene, provided that you stick to your editor's guidelines regarding what is and what isn't acceptable; the only thing to be careful of when writing SM scenes is that if you go too far, the whole thing becomes over the top and a parody of itself.

Creating an erotic ambience

When you're writing the sex scene, you need to be in a situation where:

- you're not likely to be disturbed
- you can allow your imagination free rein
- you can be completely relaxed.

Writing something in a reporter's notebook on your knee while the in-laws are over for Sunday tea is probably not the best idea! The best bet – at least until you get used to writing the sex scenes and feel more comfortable writing them – is to find yourself a place to write where you won't be disturbed, and to be partly aroused to start with. Try drinking a couple of glasses of wine and playing some good, sexy music to relax you and put you in the right mood. You could try making your own compilation tapes of music which you find a real turn-on, or burning sensuous aromatherapy oils to make you feel relaxed and sexy. Whatever works for you, use it.

KNOWING WHAT TO INCLUDE IN THE SEX SCENE

What should you include in a sex scene? As we've already seen, the golden rule is to write about things that you enjoy – that way, your enjoyment is likely to be transmitted to the reader, who will in turn enjoy reading what you've written.

Using your personal preferences

A good starting point for writing a sex scene is your own sexual relationship. What do you enjoy about making love? What are your own favourite fantasies?

Or, if you'd rather be a little more detached, think about scenes you've seen in a film or a television programme, or read in a book, and enjoyed: why did they turn you on? Think about what those scenes included. If you were writing that scene, what would you change or add, and why? Think of

- the characterisation
- the description of the characters' clothing and setting (including sound and scent)
- the level of detail in describing the sexual act

● dialogue (too much, too little, too coarse, too subtle?).

Analysing work in this way will help you work out what kind of structure, language and content would suit your own writing.

Structuring a scene

A natural structure for a sex scene is a mirror of the way things happen in real life. This is a suggestion rather than a blueprint: in fiction, as in life, not everyone will do things the same way.

Talking

Think about starting with a sexy conversation between your characters, to act as a build-up to your scene. This doesn't have to be face-to-face, but could be by telephone, or even by email, depending on your plot. It could be imaginary – though if you write an 'imaginary' scene, you need to make it feel very 'real' to your readers, or they'll be distanced from your characters.

Foreplay

The next stage is when your characters start to touch, stroke and kiss each other, on various parts of the body. If you're describing a scene where your characters are not in the same location – for example if they're having an erotic phone call or email – then the foreplay would take the form of masturbation.

The sexual act

This could include penetration – or maybe not, depending on what sexual activity you're describing. See Chapter 3 for some ideas. Remember to stick to one viewpoint only, otherwise it will confuse your readers.

Orgasm

Again, make sure you stick to one viewpoint. Also note that some erotic imprints prefer safe sex – so don't talk too much about the exchange of bodily fluids.

What follows the sexual act

More talk, possibly, or one character's thoughts.

Using body language – literally

You're writing an explicit sex scene, so talk about your characters' bodily parts, including their genital areas and erogenous zones. How does the texture and colour of their skin change, depending on which area is being touched and how aroused your characters are? What about body temperature? What does the interplay of muscles under the skin look like? How do they touch each other, and what kind of rhythm and pressure do they use?

Make sure that your anatomical details are correct – Elizabeth Coldwell, the editor of *Forum*, once received a short story containing the phrase, 'he parted her clitoris' (ouch!). If you're not sure, buy a good sex manual. Even if you are comfortable with both male and female anatomy, reading a sex manual might give you the germ of an idea which you can expand in a scene in your novel. *The Joy of Sex* by Alex Comfort is particularly good for source material.

Including more than just the sexual act

As well as describing the physical actions in the sex scene, describe what one of your characters is thinking and feeling. Again, remember to use only **one** person's viewpoint.

Don't forget **taste** and **scent** and **hearing**, when you're describing the senses, as well as **touch** and **sight**. What about the feel of clothing – or the surface on which your characters are making love? Whether it's silk sheets, cotton sheets, a Persian carpet, a perfect lawn, a beach, a big pile of autumn leaves – what does it feel like? What does the surface sound like against the character's skin? Are there any particular scents in the air?

KNOWING WHAT TO AVOID IN THE SEX SCENE

What should you avoid in the sex scene? The golden rule is very similar to that of what to include – don't write about anything that you find personally distasteful, because it will show in the manuscript and your reader will be turned off.

Excluding personal dislikes

If you prefer **vanilla sex**, *ie* something gentle which doesn't include whips and chains and spanking, that's fine. You don't have to write about bondage and SM to make your book an erotic read, although certain imprints prefer their sex scenes to be on the kinky side. Target the publisher that's right for the kind of book you want to write. If you find single-sex scenes embarrassing or distasteful, then don't include them.

Considering what editors dislike

These are usually spelled out very clearly in the publishers' guidelines. The taboo areas common to all the major publishers are:

- under-age sex

- non-consensual sex (if you decide that you really must use a rape fantasy, you need to be very careful how you handle it, and make it very obvious that it is fantasy; most editors would prefer you to avoid this)

- libel (by all means say that your character looks like a famous actor, but don't say that your character *is* that actor, and enjoys being tied up and ravished in the middle of Harrods!)

- incest

- bestiality

- turn-off words (this is quite subjective, but includes words such as slimy, pulpy, urethra *etc*)

- anything else mentioned in the publisher's guidelines as unacceptable (*eg* Headline Liaisons and Delta are not keen on 'golden rain')

Cruder isn't always ruder

Sometimes, there's a titillating shock value in having your characters use crude language. However, if one of your characters continually uses a crude expression, it's boring rather than erotic. Make sure you're rude but not crude.

PROVIDING VARIATIONS ON A THEME

Given that there are a limited number of orifices, and a limited type of things to put in those orifices, your sex scenes could very easily become identical . . . and boring.

Love's sweetest part, variety

There are many different ways of approaching your sex scene. The list of set pieces from Chapter 3 could give you some ideas. If you're writing a novel, it's likely that there will be at least one sex scene per chapter, so make sure that you vary the scenes. Remember John Donne's words: 'Love's sweetest part, variety.' That's exactly what your readers want.

Having your characters use the missionary position or the doggy position or standing up in a shower each time will bore your reader. The same is true if your characters use exactly the same foreplay each time. It's like repeating a conversation: the first time, maybe you can forgive someone's memory lapse, but the second time becomes irritating. Ring the changes – but be careful not to make it look as though your characters are working their way through the *Kama Sutra*. It's quite acceptable to use the same position more than once in a novel – just not every time or in every scene. Also remember that your characters don't have to indulge in six different sexual positions in each scene: go for quality rather than quantity.

Adding sexual tension

There's no rule that each sex scene has to end with an orgasm for one or all of the participants. If one or two scenes – especially the early ones – are interrupted before the climax, the sexual tension between your characters can make your pages sizzle. Your readers will be eager to know what happens next, and when they're finally going to go the whole way.

Using fetishes

Particularly for a male audience, think about what really turns your characters on. It could be types of materials and clothing (such as leather, lace, corsets or high-heeled shoes – don't forget that women readers also enjoy detailed description of clothing) or body parts (feet, hands, backs, breasts). If your character has a **fetish**, indulge it and describe his or her feelings for the reader. Be careful not to turn it into parody, though.

Observing the art of the possible

Although good fiction will make the reader willingly suspend their disbelief, there are limits to that willingness. Your sex scenes must be possible. If you have a male character who's five feet two and wiry and a female character who's five feet ten and twenty stone, he certainly won't be lifting her against the wall to have sex. Equally, as writer Sara Veitch says, 'If you raise a whip above your shoulder and bring it down hard, you'll virtually cut your partner in half.'

It's best to write about what you know – but that doesn't necessarily mean that you have to practise everything you write about. There are ways to cheat . . .

CHEAT'S TIPS

So how do you put across the other sex's point of view, or describe things that you've never done? Quite simply – cheat!

Using your imagination
Most erotic writers don't live out their books – apart from the fact that if they did, they'd never find the time to write about it, many erotic writers are ordinary people like you, with ordinary experiences . . . and vivid imaginations.

Asking other people for help
If you want to describe the other sex's point of view and can't even begin to imagine how they feel, ask your partner (or a close friend of the opposite sex) how they feel during intercourse. Use this as a starting point, and let your imagination take it further. Then ask him or her to read what you've written and tell you if you're on the right track. If you are, keep up the good work; if not, then you've learned something and can improve what you've just written.

Similarly, if you want to describe a sexual act that you've never done, either ask someone you know who's done it, or imagine it. For example, if your female character is making love to another woman, you don't need to have had a lesbian experience to write the scene. If you're a man, just think about your own experiences with a female lover. If you're a woman, imagine that one of the women in your scene is your partner. How does he think you feel/taste/look like?

Or is your female character is completely depilated, you don't necessarily need to try it out yourself. If you're a female writer, think how your skin feels after you've shaved your legs; or if you're a male writer, ask your partner or a close female friend.

Read widely

Finally, read widely and notice how other writers describe the sexual actions and feelings of their characters, then use that as a starting point for your own work. Though don't plagiarise; use what you've read as a springboard and keep to your own style.

CHECKLIST

Once you've written your scene, re-read it and ask yourself the following questions.

● Do you find the scene a turn-on?

● Have you described more than just the sexual act?

● Are your details automatically correct?

● Does the scene have a 'logical' structure – or, if it's cut short, does it fit in with the plot?

● Have you avoided everything on the 'things editors dislike' list?

● Have you avoided switching viewpoint?

CASE STUDIES

Kathryn uses her own experiences

Kathryn is a keen cook, and finds the presentation of food a sensual experience. She decides to include a scene in her novel which involves the lovers feeding each other as part of the foreplay. As well as the sexual action, she describes the touch and scent and taste of the foods. Her scene is a success.

Leonard isn't up to date

Leonard reads an article in the Sunday papers about the Oedipus complex. He has the bright idea of updating the Oedipus story for a modern erotic novel, and writes a synopsis based on this. Unfortunately, that means that his main theme is incest – which all the publishers' guidelines say is not acceptable as part of a plot. His idea for a book is rejected.

ASSIGNMENT

● Pick an erotic scene from a novel you've recently read. What changes would you have made to it, if you'd written it, and why?

● Write an erotic scene between a woman and her new boss.

● Rewrite the scene from the other person's point of view.

CREATING AND DEVELOPING IDEAS

Some people have a very fertile imagination and have no trouble thinking up new ideas or resolving their plots; others need help to kick-start an idea, or to break writer's block. The problem can be anything from the plot to the characters to the setting – perhaps you're not sure that your idea for a plot is more than a scene, or you're not happy with the way a character develops, or you're happy with your plot and characters but not your setting.

How can you create something new out of thin air, or develop your brief idea for a scene into a plot for an 80,000-word novel? Use the ideas below as a starting point. You may have your own sources of inspiration, from listening to music with your eyes closed, staring into an open fire, or going for a long walk on a deserted beach. Whatever works for you, use it and build on it.

FINDING INSPIRATION FOR PLOTS

Retelling an old story

There are very few 'new' plots; many books are simply retelling an old story in different words. As Kerri Sharp of Black Lace says: 'If you think about classic and fairy tales . . . take the sub-text and make it the main theme of the story.'

For example, with *Cinderella*, the basic structure of the tale is as follows.

1. The heroine experiences a large change in her life.

2. The heroine tries something new.

3. The heroine meets the hero.

4. The heroine 'loses' the hero.

5. The heroine has to adjust to her new life.

6. The hero finds the heroine again at the end.

   In *Cinderella* this works out as:

1. Cinderella's father remarries and presents her with the step-mother and step-siblings.

2. Cinderella is forced to be a servant.

3. Cinderella meets Prince Charming.

4. Cinderella leaves the ball alone.

5. Cinderella goes back to being a servant but keeps dreaming of the prince.

6. Prince Charming scours the land with the glass slipper and finds Cinderella again.

   In your novel, this could be:

1. The heroine loses her job or inherits a lot of money which frees her from the rat race.

2. The heroine is now in a different 'life' and has new sexual experiences.

3. The heroine meets the hero – who doesn't have to be the conventional tall, dark and handsome man.

4. Something happens between them so that they split up.

5. The heroine tries to go back to her old life and can't bear it.

6. The hero discovers that his quiet lover is actually the raunchy lover of his dreams and reclaims her.

Using literature other than fairy tales
Fairy tales aren't the only good sources of inspiration. There are plenty of erotic scenes in other literature. Think about the scenes between Beatrice and Benedick in *Much Ado About Nothing* or the scenes between Will Ladislaw and Dorothea Brooke in *Middlemarch* or even the scenes between Tess Durbeyfield and Angel Clare or Tess and Alec D'Urberville in *Tess of the D'Urbervilles*.

Whether you use a fairy tale or other kinds of literature as inspiration, think of what happens in the plot, and how it relates to modern life – then retell it in your own book. The circumstances of your hero and heroine may be different, their occupation and physical appearance and age may be different: but the premise behind the plot may be similar.

Gaining visual inspiration
If your imagination is captured more by visual elements than by reading, then watch television and film adaptations of novels and plays. What creates the sexual charge between the characters? How is it shown on the screen – and how can you transfer a similar charge to your own work?

Using dreams and daydreams
Keep a pen and paper by your bed. If you wake up from a very vivid and interesting dream, write it down – you may be able to use part of it later, either in a single scene or as the basis for a complete plot. Remember, though, to avoid putting it into your novel as a dream. The dream-sequence is unpopular with some editors.

Observing people
As well as helping to develop characters, observing people can help you to build a plot. Maybe an attractive man or woman catches your eye in the street. What is he or she really like? Where is he or she going, and why? (That could give you your characters and your plot, in one fell swoop.)

Eliza Down wrote a novel which was sparked off by seeing a couple together in the woods, when she'd stayed with a friend for the weekend and visited a local stately home. The way they were acting gave her an idea for a scene, which developed into a fully-fledged novel.

Conversations with friends

It's often said that everyone has a book in them; but not everyone wants to write a novel. Even so, if your friends know that you write, they'll often suggest things to you which might be useful for a plot – for example, they may have had a vivid dream which you can use as the basis of a scene or even a whole novel.

Conversations following dinner parties, when everyone's mellow and the topic rambles, are also useful to help you build plots. For example, what would you or your friends do after winning the jackpot on the lottery or inheriting a large sum of money? How could that be turned into an erotic situation? If you're having trouble with the plot of your novel, you could always turn the conversation round to that, and see what kind of ideas your friends have for resolving your plot. Their suggestions will usually be the kind of things they enjoy reading about, so it's useful feedback.

Using the small ads in your local newspaper

There are bound to be some unusual ads in the back pages of your local newspaper. Who placed them, and why? (Character plus motivation equals plot – or at least the beginnings of one.)

If one of your characters placed an ad in a newspaper (though not a 'contact' ad – as we've already seen, that's been done to death), what kind of ads would surround it? What kind of language would your character use and why?

DEVELOPING YOUR CHARACTERS

Observing people

If you're out shopping, or on the bus, or sitting at a pavement café or even walking round a stately home or museum on a Sunday afternoon, watch the people round you. They can be inspiring – the way they look, the way they move, mannerisms, the way they greet other people and the way they interact with their surroundings. Many authors keep a notebook specifically to jot down notes for potential characters – which usually end up as a combination of one person's hair, another's eyes, another's smile and so forth.

Using dreams and daydreams

We've all dreamed about Prince Charming or a beautiful princess, or had a crush on an actor, actress or musician. But what if you met the man or woman of your dreams – how would you feel? How would they react to you? Would it cause any difficulties in your life?

Or if you could swap places with someone, who would you choose? What elements of that person's character do you find attractive, and why?

Conservations with friends

This is akin to asking your audience what they want. Who are their sexual heroes, and what draws them to these men or women? Is it their physical appearance, or a particular attribute of their character? What kind of characters do they enjoy reading about, and why? Conversely, do any characters turn·them off? If so, why? It's useful to be aware of elements to avoid as well as things to include.

Using small ads in the local newspaper

Start with the 'find a partner' ads. What sort of person placed that ad? What kind of person are they looking for? What kind of person might reply, and why?

The births, marriages and deaths columns are also useful as a source of names (though do remember to split the first name from the surname. Using real names could land you with a libel action.)

FINDING NEW SETTINGS

Keeping a cuttings file

Keep a file of cuttings of places which catch your eye – whether it's a property, a location or a garden. If you decide to put a scene in your book about a castle in Scotland or a windmill in Norfolk, it will help to have a picture if you haven't actually visited those places.

Rich sources for cuttings include:

- *magazines* – particularly the monthly and more upmarket ones, and magazines aimed at people renovating period homes

- *newspapers* – particularly the property pages of the broadsheets at the weekends, and the lifestyle features in their magazines

- *hotel brochures*

- *tourist guides*

- *holiday brochures*

- *the window of estate agents* dealing in upmarket properties (ask for brochures of any place that takes your fancy – this doesn't have to be in your home area).

- *calendars* – based on local landscapes.

Watching films and television programmes

This could be anything from watching one of the holiday programmes or a documentary about a foreign location, to falling in love with a house in a TV drama. If something catches your eye, video it and use it as a springboard for the setting in your novel.

Using new experiences

Whatever your new experience is, whether it's a visit to an optician, a trip to a stately home, or starting evening classes in Spanish, think of its potential as an erotic setting. Who could your characters meet in that setting? What could happen?

Using real-life situations

This could be anything from your computer in the office going wrong and an engineer coming to fix it, to being trapped in a lift with an incredibly attractive man or woman, to renovating a house. What are the erotic possibilities of the situation? What kind of events would happen with that kind of backdrop?

Using holidays

Holidays – particularly those taken abroad – are great for settings. Take notes about the climate, the surroundings (house styles, plants, animals) and the sort of people around you. Take photographs to help refresh your memory when you're back home a few months later, and want to use your holiday as the basis of a setting.

Friends' holidays, too, are a useful source for settings, particularly if your friends have gone to an exotic location or, for example, know an area of France particularly well. Your friends will have anecdotes, memories and photographs which can all be used for the setting of your novel; if your friends know the area particularly well, they can also give you more information about local colour which will help to make your book's setting more vivid.

PUTTING A NEW TWIST ON OVERUSED IDEAS

As we're already seen, certain plots and settings have been done to death. But you can nearly always place a new twist on old ideas, if you try hard enough.

Settings

For example, take the setting of a harem. Supposing you turn it the other way round and write a scene where your female character fantasies what it would be like to be a sultan – or to have a male harem? That's more interesting than the bog-standard and over-used idea of a woman being part of a harem.

Plots

Or there's the plot of someone placing or answering an ad in a contact magazine – supposing your character sends the ad or the reply to the wrong place? What happens if his or her mail is opened by the wrong person who has, say, the same initial and surname? Or maybe the mail is delivered to the wrong address – to a house with the same number and road name, but a slightly different postcode, and there is no contact name on the envelope: what could be the consequences?

Adding layers of intrigue

Then there is the 'initiation' type novel – particularly the sub-genre of the 'secret erotic society' recruiting a new member, which is beginning to be overused. Supposing that in your novel, James 'recruits' Sarah, not realising that Sarah is actually much higher up in the same society and is playing a part while she checks that James' recruitment methods are appropriate? It's more interesting for your readers than the simple plot of 'James recruits Sarah'. You could add yet another layer of intrigue, in that Sarah herself is being tested for promotion, or maybe being groomed to be the head of the society.

EMPLOYING THE 'WHAT IF . . . ?' METHOD

What if . . . ? is a method of either garnering a new plot from another one, or taking a plot further.

Read widely, watch films and plays, listen to plays and short stories on the radio. Think of something you enjoyed reading or watching or listening to – then ask yourself 'what if' *x* had happened instead of *y*, in the plot.

For example, if we take *Wuthering Heights* – what did Heathcliff do during his absence? Where did he go? Or if he'd stayed at Wuthering Heights instead of going off to make his fortune – what would have happened then? Would he have married Cathy? What would Hindley have done? The whole plot of the novel would have been different.

Or *Alice in Wonderland* – supposing that when she ate or drank something, instead of growing or shrinking, she changed sex? Or she became a shape-shifter, actually turning into a white rabbit or a dormouse or a Cheshire cat? (NB editors are not keen on mixing fantasy with erotica – this example is to show the method rather than the content.)

Applying the parallel universe theory

'What if . . . ?' can be likened to the parallel universe theory: the possibilities are only limited by your imagination. In one story, Peter and Jane meet at a masked party and end up going back to Peter's flat to make love. What if Jane doesn't actually make it to the party, so they never meet – what does Jane do instead, and who does she meet? Still taking the party as the central point, Peter and Jane meet at a party and make a rendezvous for later. Unknown to them, another couple have agreed to meet at the same time and the same place. What if Peter and the other woman are both late – and Jane ends up making love with the other man? A fourth possibility is that Peter and Jane both go to the party, but meet different people and go home with them instead.

The list of possible variations could go on and on. Keep asking 'what if . . . ?', and you'll find that a plot will eventually start to take shape.

CHECKLIST

● Start a notebook for ideas and keep a small version with you; transfer your notes periodically to your main notebook. That way, if you lose your notebook, you'll have a back-up and you won't have lost everything.

● Check your cuttings file every week, and make a note of which ones you've already used. Put these in a separate section, not to be used for at least five books.

● When you come to a sticking point in your story (even at the beginning), ask yourself 'what if . . . ?'.

● Look at your idea for a plot. Is it really an original angle on an old theme? If it isn't original, start asking yourself 'what if . . . ?' until it is.

CASE STUDIES

Mandy finds inspiration in a junk shop

Mandy is on holiday at a seaside town in England. On one particularly wet day, she spends her time browsing through the local junkshops and bric-a-brac shops and discovers a beautiful amber pendant. She buys it. She wonders who bought it originally, who that person gave it to, and why? Using the 'what if . . . ?' method she develops an idea for a plot, based round the pendant.

Neil keeps a notebook

Neil keeps a notebook, subdivided into sections for ideas for plots, characters, settings and scenes. If he overhears a snatch of intriguing conversation on the bus or in the pub, he writes it down, using it later as a springboard for a scene in his novel. He finds that using something rooted in real life helps him to keep his characters and his action more believable.

ASSIGNMENT

Try to think of at least three new ways of how you could use a health club in a novel.

8
Submitting Your Manuscript

MAKING SURE IT'S THE RIGHT KIND OF MATERIAL

Before you send anything to a publisher, always check that you're submitting the right kind of material for that publisher's list – otherwise you're wasting your time and money, as well as wasting the editor's time. There's no point in sending an erotic novel to Mills and Boon, or a novel aimed at a female audience to Nexus, because it simply won't be suitable for their list. Always do your homework before you submit a novel. Make sure that you've fulfilled the editorial requirements regarding length and content, and that you've read the editor's guidelines and haven't included anything which falls outside those guidelines.

PUTTING YOUR SUBMISSION TOGETHER

When you send a novel to a publisher for consideration, your submission needs to include:

* a covering letter
* an SAE
* either the synopsis and the first three chapters of your novel, or the synopsis and the full manuscript.

Send these in an envelope or a wallet file; if you prefer, you can put an elastic band round your manuscript to keep it together. Don't staple chapters together or use ring-binders, because it makes it difficult for the editor to read or make comments, although paper-clipping chapters together is fine.

Presenting your manuscript
Some of the advice below may seem blindingly obvious, and many

books on creative writing contain similar advice to new writers – but despite that, editors still receive many poorly-presented manuscripts.

Poor presentation is an immediate turn-off. Your manuscript might join another 50 on the slush pile in a particular week, and a busy editor is likely to give more time to a neat manuscript than to a dog-eared, coffee-stained bundle which looks as if it's already been rejected by a dozen publishers.

Important points to note
Your manuscript should always:

- be typed (or printed in letter-quality) on A4 paper

- be presented in double spacing (that is, leave a blank line between each line of text)

- have at least a two-centimetre margin on all four sides of the paper – a three-centimetre left-hand margin is probably better

- have consecutive page numbers in the top right-hand corner (and note that new chapters do not start at page one again), together with your name and the manuscript title

- start the first paragraph of a chapter full out to the left margin

- start other paragraphs indented by five spaces, with no extra lines between paragraphs (unless there is a 'scene' break, in which case leave an extra line after the paragraph of the last scene, and start the paragraph of the new scene full out to the left margin).

See Figure 8 on page 94 for a sample layout.

The first page, or front sheet, should always contain:

- the title of the manuscript
- your name
- your pseudonym (if any)
- your address
- your telephone number
- the approximate word-count of your novel.

CHAPTER ONE

'Bloody hell, Charlie, some people have all the luck!' Vanessa lifted her glass up in a salute. 'I wish I had a rich great-great-uncle who'd leave me a fortune.'

'You'd spend it all on shoes,' Ralph, her husband, said with a grin.

'Huh.' Vanessa ignored him and took a swig of wine. 'So what are you going to do with the money, Charlie?'

'The first thing is, I'm chucking in my job.' Charlotte beamed. 'I'm really looking forward to that, believe me. Handing in my notice . . . It's going to be fantastic.'

'Oh?' Simeon, noticing the look in her violet eyes, was intrigued. 'What are you plotting, Charlie?'

She grinned, her face dimpling as she looked at him. 'What makes you think I'm plotting, Sim?'

'Your face gives you away,' he informed her. 'It's full of mischief.'

'What, me? Charlotte "call-me-responsible" Fraser?' she asked with a chuckle.

'Yes, you,' Simeon said, laughing back. 'You might be respectable and responsible at work, but we've been your friends for years. We know what you're really like!'

'I haven't danced naked on tabletops for . . . ooh, it must be all of 30 years,' she teased.

Simeon shook his head. 'You know what I mean, Charlie. You're not an exhibitionist – but you're not exactly Miss Prissy Prim-and-Proper either, are you?'

'No, I suppose you're right.' She spread her hands. 'Okay, I'll tell you – provided that you all promise me that you won't leak this, no matter who asks you. I don't want anything ruining the impact.'

Fig. 8. Sample manuscript layout.

Pamela Rochford/Dangerous Consequences/page 1

DANGEROUS CONSEQUENCES

by

PAMELA ROCHFORD

1 THE STREET

NEWTOWN

AB1 2CD

TELEPHONE 01234 567890

Approx 75,000 words

Fig. 9. Sample front sheet layout.

See Figure 9 above for a sample layout.

Other general points to note

- New chapters *always* begin on a new page, with the first paragraph starting full out to the left-hand margin.

- If there are any scribbles, tipp-ex or coffee stains on pages, retype them.

- If your manuscript is dog-eared from rejections, retype it – first appearances count.

- Only send your manuscript to one publisher at a time – it could cause problems if both editors like it!

- Always use a new ribbon or printer cartridge; if your toner or drum needs changing, do it before you print out your manuscript.

Checking grammar and spelling

- Make sure that your grammar and spelling are correct.

- Ask a friend to check your manuscript in draft, if you're in any doubt.

- If you use a word-processor, use the spell-check function – even if you're a brilliant speller, it's very easy to make a typing mistake. (Remember that spell-check programs only check the spelling of a word, not that you've typed the right word – you might have typed 'sage' instead of 'safe', which the spell check program will assume is correctly spelled, so read your manuscript through as well.)

Checking your publisher's house style

- Do they prefer words ending in *-ise* or *-ize*?

- Do they like past participles ending in -ed, or do they prefer -t endings where possible? (for example, leant, learnt, burnt or leaned, learned, burned?).

- Do they like new paragraphs to be indented, or do they like all paragraphs to be full against the left-hand margin, with extra lines between paragraphs?

- Do they use single or double speech marks? (Most publishers prefer single.)

- Do they like song titles *etc* underlined or in speech marks? Is there a difference between titles of films, books or plays and titles of songs?

- What about breaks within chapters (for example, when changing the scene)? Do the publishers want them marked by three asterisks, or should there be just an extra line space to denote the break in the chapter?

- What about unfinished sentences, or sentences which are broken off or interrupted – do they want a dash or ellipsis (three points, that is, . . .)?

- What about titles and acronyms, for example Dr or NATO? Do they want stops in them or not?

Checking you have the right number of words
Make sure that you're submitting the right number of words (or potentially, in the case of a synopsis and sample chapters for a novel). If someone wants 80,000 words or more, there's no point in sending them a 50,000-word novel. Similarly, if they specify 60,000 words, don't send them a 100,000-word novel.

STRUCTURING THE COVERING LETTER

Always make your covering letter personal. Address it to the right person rather than just to Dear Sir/Madam in 'the editorial department'. Think about the mail you receive – you read letters addressed to you more carefully than you read a letter addressed to 'Dear Customer' or 'Dear Householder', and the same is true of editors. If you've done your homework, it will count in your favour.

The editors of various imprints are usually listed in books such as the *Writers' and Artists' Yearbook* or *The Writer's Handbook* – but, as people do change jobs, it's worthwhile checking by phone, the first time, just to make sure that you're writing to the right person.

Keep your letter brief. Say what you're submitting for their consideration (including the title and approximate word-count) and ask for comments re its unsuitability *if* the editor has time – and thank them for spending the time to read your manuscript. Politeness matters. Always type your name at the bottom of the letter, even if your signature is legible.

Things to avoid

- 'My friend/husband/mother/neighbour/second cousin twice removed read it and thought that it was really good' (apart from the fact that someone close to you is likely to be biased, an editor doesn't need to be told his or her job).

- 'There's so much rubbish around, I thought I could write better' (insulting and likely to annoy an editor – would you give a contract to someone who tells you that you produce rubbish and he or she could do better?).

- Telling your life story, reasons for writing the book or your financial situation (it's not relevant to your book).

- Asking how much they'll pay you for it – don't assume acceptance, even if you've had novels accepted by other publishers. Your style might be right for one imprint but not for another.

See Figure 10 on page 99 for an example covering letter.

LOOKING AT CVS AND PSEUDONYMS

Sending a CV

If you've already had some relevant success in publishing – which means short stories or novels accepted in a related genre, not a letter in the local paper or a 'true-life story' in a magazine – it's sometimes helpful to send a CV with your submission.

Once you've had a novel accepted, your publisher or agent may ask for a CV, for publicity purposes. Keep it simple and to the point. Publishers, unlike potential employers, are not interested in your employment history, exactly which exams you've taken and the grades you achieved. They're more interested in unusual hobbies or unusual things about you (for example that you're one of triplets, or you build dry-stone walls, or that you spent a year sheep-shearing in New Zealand) which can help to gain publicity for your book.

An example structure for a CV is in Figure 11 on page 100.

A N Author
1 The Street
Anytown
AB1 2CD

Mr J Bloggs
The Erotic Publishing Company
1 The Road
Anycity
EF3 4GH

1 September 199x

Dear Mr Bloggs,

Please find enclosed the synopsis and first three chapters of an 80,000-word novel, *Night Moves*, for your consideration.

If it is not suitable, I would appreciate any comments you could make.

Thank you for your time. I enclose an SAE.

Yours sincerely

A N Author

A N Author

Fig. 10. Example of a covering letter.

Using a pseudonym

If you only want to work for one publisher and you don't mind using your real name, then that's fine. If you'd rather use a pseudonym – meaning that you can use your own name for mainstream fiction or articles – that's perfectly acceptable. Note that if you write for several publishers, they'll usually like you to use a separate pseudonym for each imprint.

Pick your pseudonym in the same way that you pick a character's

CURRICULUM VITAE

Name	Jane Smith (née Brown)
Born	January 1, 1965, London
Educated	London Grammar School:
	10 O levels, 3 A levels
	University of Manchester,
	BA Hons (IIi) English, 1986
Other professional qualifications	Diploma in Marketing, 1990

Published work

Short stories: Fifteen short stories published since 1990 in *Forum, For Women* and *Desire.*
Novels: Shadowed Obsession, Headline, 1994 (as Charmaine Jones)
Dark Challenge, Black Lace, 1995 (as Lucy Rivers)
Vampire Passion, NEL, due out 1998 (as Marilyn Bloggs)

Other information

I live in a village just outside Manchester with my husband Joe, my children (Peter, aged 3 and Paul, aged 13 months) and two cats. I work part-time as a copy-editor for a local advertising agency and am also on the board of the local playgroup.

My interests include reading, cinema, theatre, aerobics and archery.

Fig. 11. Sample CV.

name – and don't make up a name with an erotic connotation. 'Lucy Spanks' sounds more like ridicule than anything else, and your editor will ask you to rethink your pseudonym – if your unsolicited manuscript under that name gets that far.

WAITING FOR A REPLY – AND WHEN TO CHASE

Don't expect an answer within a week. As erotica becomes a more and more popular genre, publishers have to wade through more and more manuscripts. It takes time to read all this material.

Some publishers send out acknowledgement postcards. If you just want to make sure that your MS has arrived, attach a self-addressed (and stamped) postcard saying 'I confirm that [write in your manuscript name here] has arrived and we will be in touch as soon as possible' and ask in your letter if they will send the postcard to you so that you know your manuscript has arrived.

You *should* hear within three months – if you haven't heard by then, it's worth writing a short and *polite* letter expressing your concern and asking for the return of your MS if it's unsuitable.

Above all, don't phone and hassle the editors. They're busy, and the time they spent on the phone to you could have been better spent reading a manuscript.

CHECKLIST

- Make sure that your manuscript is printed in double spacing with wide margins.

- Check your page numbers – make sure that they're consecutive.

- Check your manuscript for typing mistakes and reprint corrected pages if necessary.

- Enclose an SAE with your submission.

CASE STUDIES

Paul makes false economies

Paul wants to keep his expenses to a minimum, so he doesn't replace his typewriter ribbons when typing up his sample chapters and synopsis. As a result his typescript is so faint that it's barely legible. He is surprised when his manuscript is rejected.

Rebecca keeps it brief

Rebecca's covering letter is short, polite, and to the point. She also remembers to enclose an SAE. Although her first manuscript is not up to the required standard, the editor is impressed with her letter and writes back with encouragement and advice about how to improve her next submission.

ASSIGNMENT

Write your CV, based on the example in Figure 11.

9
Learning From Experience

DEALING WITH REJECTION LETTERS

Seeing a thick envelope lying on the doormat, addressed in your own handwriting, is one of the worst things in the world for a writer, because it almost always heralds a rejection slip and the return of your manuscript.

Rejection hurts. Of course you're going to be upset about it. But don't brood for too long – throw the whole thing into a corner and sulk about it for a day at most, then pick it up again and read the editor's comments. Editors are always on the lookout for new talent and if they think you have potential, they'll encourage you, so take their comments on board. If they ask you to try again, it's not just a polite way of telling you to go away – they're interested. So read what they have to say about why your manuscript wasn't right for them, and *do something about it.*

Once you've read their comments take one of the following three positive steps.

1. Revamp your manuscript and resubmit it, if appropriate.

2. Send if off to someone else, if you've sent the wrong sort of material.

3. Put it to one side, take the comments on board and start writing your next book.

Learning from experience

Look on a rejection letter as a learning experience. Think of other things you've learned to do in the past – for example, to walk, to ride a bike, to drive a car, to swim or to use a typewriter. You weren't perfect immediately with any of those skills; similarly,

103

don't expect your writing to be perfect (and accepted) immediately. You'll improve with practice, and if you persist and take note of any criticism and advice, you'll eventually succeed in being published.

The rejection letter may contain something to help you to improve – for example, the editor may tell you what's wrong with the manuscript and make suggestions for changes, or alert you to problem areas to help you with your next manuscript. If you are given such help, use it.

Don't be disheartened
If you receive what seems like a standard 'thank you for offering your book to us but it is not suitable for our list' letter, don't be disheartened. It's possible that your manuscript arrived when the editorial department was inundated with unsolicited manuscripts and the editor .simply hasn't had time to explain why your manuscript was unsuitable. In this case, go back to the drawing board. Look at the guidelines and analyse a couple of novels published by that imprint. Then look at your novel: where are you falling short of the standard? If you're not sure, it might be worth asking a friend to help, or submitting your manuscript to a reading service such as that provided by the Guild of Erotic Writers.

Deciding whether erotic writing is for you

If you've received several rejection slips, be honest with yourself. Are you really writing the genre that suits you best? If you're not comfortable reading or writing erotic novels, but you like writing books with historical settings, you might be a better saga-writer than an erotic writer. Or maybe you enjoy reading or writing plots with more of a mystery element than a sexy element, and you'd be better working as a thriller-writer.

Keeping on the lookout for salvage

Never throw a rejected book away. It may have salvageable material. You may be able to revamp elements of it when you've written more and are more sure of your ability.

REWRITING TO YOUR EDITOR'S REQUIREMENTS

Sometimes a rejection letter isn't a complete rejection. If the editor says what was wrong with the story, that's a good indication that he or she thinks that you have potential. In these cases, ring the editor and ask if you can resubmit your revised manuscript.

Sometimes the answer will be no – that particular idea might be unworkable, even with revision. If your manuscript falls into this category, ask if you can submit another idea – and make sure that you avoid the problems of your last manuscript in your next submission.

If the answer is yes, your idea might be suitable after revision, then start working on your manuscript. Go through what the editor has said needs revising, and make the changes that he or she suggests. Common areas where rewrites are needed include:

- *plots* – either too complex or too simple

- *setting* – overused, or not enough erotic potential

- *viewpoint* – you need to stick to *one* person's point of view per scene. Don't mix it – your readers will be confused. And never, ever change viewpoint in a flashback.

AVOIDING EDITORIAL PET HATES

The question 'what are your pet hates?' elicited the following replies from the top editors of erotica.

> Sleazy crime – drug smuggling, blackmail, murder, prostitution, extortion or anything else more at home in *The Sweeney*. 'Sex as currency' – using sex as a means to an end for financial gain or to get out of trouble; this renders the sex as perfunctory. Complete unsolicited manuscripts arriving without synopses. (Kerri Sharp, Black Lace)

> As an editor, I have frequently read material which I might have taken on if only the sample hadn't featured one of my pet hates. If, for example, you submitted to me a novel which opened with a Mile High Club bonk, a scene of the heroine appraising her nude body in a mirror ('not bad for her age, mused Samantha') or a dream sequence, I'd probably reject out of personal prejudice no matter how brilliant your treatment. (Mike Bailey, Headline – quoted from *Teach Yourself Writing Erotic Fiction*)

Authors who haven't done their homework and send manuscripts which don't meet the guidelines. Illiterate manuscripts and subliterate writing. (Nick Austin, NEL)

Scenes which contain things that sound as if they hurt – pleasure as pain is acceptable as part of an erotic novel, but it's a turn-off if it goes too far. Unattractive-sounding underwear (particularly flesh-coloured). Turn-off words such as 'gusset'. (Helen Pisano, X Libris)

People who request guidelines then submit a story which completely ignores them. Writers who are paranoid about your stealing their ideas and obsessively copyrighting them – usually these are ideas which are not worth stealing in the first place, and editors of erotica don't rip people off. Writers who won't take criticism or guidance, and submit work which still has the same faults I pointed out when I sent their first manuscript back. (Elizabeth Coldwell, editor of *Forum* magazine)

People who don't research the market and send me unsuitable manuscripts or ask me if I will act as their agent. Covering letters which are full of 'herewith and hereunder' – it usually means that the manuscript will be unreadable, too. People who can't write a sensible covering letter – such as the one I received saying, 'I am a freelance out-of-work journalist and I want to write a pronographic [sic] novel.' (Josephine Scott, Olympia)

Authors who get too carried away with corporal punishment scenes, making them unrealistic and monotonous. Manuscripts which don't have imaginative sexual encounters or colourful characters. (Adrian Wilkins, Chimera)

The same pet hates crop up again and again. It's easy to avoid all these by:

- reading widely in your chosen target imprint so that you're familiar with the kind of books that the editor publishes

- sending for the imprint's guidelines – and reading them thoroughly

- making sure that your work adheres to those guidelines

- being careful with your punctuation, grammar, spelling and language.

IMPROVING YOUR WRITING

Keeping a notebook with you
There are three specific areas where a notebook is useful:

- for describing scenes
- for taking down snatches of dialogue (either overheard or imagined)
- for describing someone whose appearance has caught your attention in the street.

Your notes may spark off an idea for a book or story – or may be helpful when you're in the middle of a book.

Reading and analysing as much as you can
You'll soon discover what your favourite type of erotica is – this will be the sort you'll write best, too.

Analyse what you like and don't like about the erotic writing you read – which elements do you like or dislike most?

- character (the types, the number of characters and the viewpoint used)
- plot (are there too many twists or not enough?)
- description (is it detailed or brief?)
- dialogue (how much is there? how often does it appear in a scene?)
- style (are long or short sentences used; if a mixture, what sort of proportion?)
- pace (is it rich and stately; or fast and furious?)
- vocabulary and language.

Watching your grammar and spelling
If you know that this is your weak spot, buy one of the grammar books on the market or a good dictionary (or use a word-processing program which has a spell-checker, but watch out for the wrong words spelled correctly!).

If you get confused between different spellings of the same-sounding word, buy a spelling dictionary to help – or ask a friend who's good at English to help you.

Being honest with yourself

One of the best ways of self-criticism is to leave your finished story for a couple of weeks, then go back and re-read it when it's no longer fresh in your mind. You'll be able to see the weaknesses more easily, reading what you actually wrote instead of what you intended to write.

Rewriting your book when you've finished the first draft

Do as many rewrites as you feel are necessary. Some authors rewrite their novels five or six times; others work on the first and third drafts at the same time (for example, chapter one might have been revised twice while they're still writing chapter eight). However, whatever you do, don't write out the freshness of your first draft. Spending hours and hours deciding on whether to use a full stop or a semi-colon won't help you much.

When you rewrite, have a specific aim in mind. You might find it helpful to do several different rewrites, concentrating on a different aspect each time: for example, working on the plot in the first revision, your prose on the second, and your dialogue on the third.

DEALING WITH WRITER'S BLOCK

This happens to every author, at some point. You sit in front of a blank piece of paper (or a blank computer screen) and your brain refuses to tell you what comes next.

The important thing is – *don't panic!* It will break. It might take a few minutes, hours, days or weeks, but it *will* break.

Try some of the following recognised ways to help break writer's block.

- Have a long scented bath, with a glass of wine and some good music.

- Go for a walk.

- Have a cup of coffee and read the paper.

- Forget the book and do something different – maybe a mundane job you've been avoiding.

- Ring a friend – and don't talk about anything to do with the book.

- Go shopping.

- Put the book on ice for a while and work on something else.

Eventually, you'll start writing again – usually when you're nowhere near a piece of paper!

CHECKLIST

- Re-read your work with a critical eye; look out for the areas which you know are your weak points and revise where necessary.

- Are you happy that your revised draft is more suited to your target market?

- Make sure that you have followed any editorial advice from previous submissions. If necessary, ask someone else to read it and check for you.

- Check your work carefully to make sure that you've avoided the editor's pet hates.

CASE STUDIES

Susan rejects editorial advice

Susan is a 45-year-old secretary who has a very good grasp of grammar, punctuation and spelling, and often corrects her boss's letters at work. She has spent the past six months writing an erotic novel in her spare time. Her manuscript has just been returned by the editor with suggestions for improvement. Susan refuses to consider the editor's comments, because she thinks that her idea is fine as it is and she doesn't need to revise it or improve her writing. She sends it, unaltered, to another publisher and is annoyed to receive another rejection letter.

Terry spends time analysing

Terry has just had his third submission rejected. He decides that, rather than working on his fourth idea, he will spend the next month reading half a dozen novels in his chosen imprint. After analysing them, he can see the differences between his work and a successful novel. He thinks that, with revision, his first idea might be acceptable. He revises his first synopsis and sample chapters, tightening the writing, improving the interaction between his characters and writing the sex scenes more sensually. His new covering letter explains that this is a resubmission but that he has revised the manuscript considerably after analysing it, together with several already published novels. This time, his proposal is accepted.

ASSIGNMENT

Go through a piece of your most recent erotic writing, checking it for editorial hates. Be honest with yourself and write a list of the points which could be improved (or, if you'd rather, ask a friend to check it for you). Then use that list to revise your original draft.

10
After Acceptance – What Now?

Your first acceptance letter is a real moment of celebration. All that hard work has paid off, and someone apart from your family and friends finally believes in your ability as a writer. It's a moment to be savoured. But once you've drunk the champagne and celebrated with your friends and family – what then?

LOOKING AT CONTRACTS

Once you've had a book accepted – whether it's on the strength of your synopsis and first three chapters, or the complete manuscript – the publisher will send you a **contract**. If you have an agent he or she will read through the contract and ensure that you're getting the best deal, but it's still worth reading it through yourself.

Reading through the contract
Some contracts are written in plain English and others are written in more formal legal language, but the contents are fairly standard between the publishers.

The most important points are:

Delivery date
This is the date when you need to deliver the manuscript to the publisher; it's usually agreed between you or your agent and the editor before the contract is drafted. Before you agree to a date, make sure that it's realistic. if you write quickly and know that you only need two months to complete the novel, then agree a date for two months ahead; if you need more time, then agree a delivery date that's further away.

Whatever you agree with the publisher, make sure that you stick to it. Editors don't tend to commission more books from authors who don't deliver. If you think that there's any chance you'll miss

111

the deadline – for example, you have a prolonged illness – then speak to your editor as soon as possible to explain the situation and renegotiate the deadline. Editors are always understanding if there's a real problem – provided that you keep them informed at the earliest opportunity.

Word-count

This is often specified as being between an upper and lower limit. if you go below the limit, the publisher will ask you for a rewrite (and is unlikely to accept more work from you, because asking you to rewrite the book means that they'll have to change their production schedules and maybe ask another author to deliver early). If you go over the word limit, the publisher will need to ask a copy-editor to take out large chunks; again, this costs time and money. So stick to the agreed limits for the word-count.

Title

This is the eventual title of your book. Once you've had more than one book accepted by that publisher then, depending on your relationship with the editor, the title in the contract might be a working title rather than the final one.

Payment

Advance payment is usually divided into a third on signature of the contract, a third on delivery, and a third on publication. Some publishers divide the advance into two: half on signature and half on publication. Royalties – that is, a percentage of the cover price of your book – will be payable once or twice a year, once you've sold enough copies to cover the cost of your advance.

Royalties are not payable on the copies given to you, or on copies given to reviewers. An amount – usually 25 per cent for paperbacks – is held back at each royalty statement to cover returns (ie books which bookshops haven't sold and decide to return to the publisher).

Note also that some royalties are payable on a 'net receipt' basis (ie the amount that the publisher receives from the bookseller, as opposed to the cover price), depending on the type of discount given to the bookseller and whether it's a home or overseas sale.

Royalties will also be payable on subsidiary sales, such as book club editions, audio tapes and editions printed by a publisher in another country (usually America or Australia).

Publication date
Don't expect the book to be on the shelves of your local bookshop within a month of delivering your manuscript. Publishers work with long lead times, and the publication date is likely to be around a year after you deliver the finished manuscript.

Your next book
There may be a clause saying that the publisher wishes to reserve the right to publish your next book under that particular pseudonym or your real name. Unfortunately, this doesn't mean that they will actually publish it – they just want the chance to consider it first. If they reject it, you'll be free to send it elsewhere, though probably under a different pseudonym.

Free copies
As part of your remuneration, the publisher will send you a number of free copies of your book, a couple of weeks before publication date. Royalties are not payable on these.

Clarifying the contract
If there's anything that you don't understand in the contract, ask your editor for clarification. If you are a member of the Society of Authors, it's worth taking advantage of their contract-reading service, where they will read any contract and offer advice free of charge.

UNDERSTANDING PROOFS, BLURBS AND ILLUSTRATIONS

Receiving proofs
Once you've delivered the manuscript, it goes to the **copy-editor**. Any typing errors, spelling mistakes and grammatical errors will be picked up by the copy-editor, along with any deviations from house style (for example, if you've used double quote marks instead of single quote marks, or you've used -ed endings and they prefer -t endings where possible). The copy-editor will also query anything that might be incorrect, such as the habitat of particular flora and fauna, or whether certain mineral types are found together – or even whether some of your scenes are physically possible (for example, it's unlikely that your hero will be able to tie his own wrists in a bondage scene, and loosen them afterwards). Then the

marked-up manuscript goes to the **typesetter**, and the first **proofs** are produced.

The publisher will then send proofs to you for correction, telling you the latest date when he or she needs comments. The proofs will look almost exactly the same as the finished book, although there will be two 'pages' on each sheet of A4 paper. This is your chance to go through the proofs and pick up any errors; or you may choose to leave it all in the hands of the publisher's proofreader (who will go through the manuscript checking for corrections, whether you give any comments or not). Don't make full-scale changes to the text at this stage, or you'll be charged for the cost of resetting those pages.

It's worth asking for the return of your original manuscript, so you can see where the copy-editor has made changes; this will help you with future books, because you'll become more familiar with the publisher's house style and also be aware of any stylistic problems you have (such as 'throat-clearing' or misuse of commas).

Writing the blurb

At the same time as the copy-editing stage, either the copy-editor or the editor will write the wording for the back of the book-jacket – known as the **blurb**. The aim of the blurb is to give an idea of the plot (without giving too much away) and a sample of the book's contents, usually including a piece of dialogue. If you've written a good selling synopsis, part of it may be used as your book's blurb.

The editor will send the blurb to you for approval. You have the chance to make any changes here, if you really don't like what they've written, but usually the blurb-writer has a lot of experience and knows what sells in their market.

Choosing illustrations

Once the blurb has been approved, the editor will choose the **cover illustration**, have everything set, and then send you a copy. If you really hate the illustration, you may be able to negotiate changes; however, it's worth remembering that the publisher is likely to have done a great deal of market research and found out the sort of covers that their target readers like, so the publisher will have a better idea of what kind of illustration helps to sell a book.

WORKING UP YOUR NEXT SUBMISSION

Depending on your relationship with the editor, you may be asked only to send one sample chapter, together with the synopsis, for your next submission. Remember that there are no guarantees of acceptance – established authors still have ideas for books rejected by their publishers – and to be polite and patient, as with a first submission. The good news is that once you've had a book published, you'll avoid that publisher's slush pile in the future, so you have a better chance of an acceptance.

KEEPING RECORDS

There are two particular sets of records you need to keep.

1. Your own records of submissions, so you know what's been sent where, and the reaction of the publisher

2. Records of income and expenditure, for tax purposes.

Recording submissions

Keep a note of what you've sent to which publisher, when, and their reaction. This will save you from the embarrassing situation of sending a novel to a publisher, having it rejected, having it rejected by another three, and then sending it back to the first one because you'd forgotten that you'd already had it rejected by them.

A simple columnar record will do. See Figure 12 for an example. Including a 'results' column has the added advantage of showing you at a glance the main reason why you've been rejected. If you've had three novels rejected for having too complex a plot, or too thin a plot, you know one of the areas you need to work on before you submit any further ideas.

Date	Title	Pseudonym	To	Result
1.1.199x	*The Master*	Jane Bloggs	Headline	No – plot not exciting enough. Try a different book
1.3.199x	*Dark Desires*	June Smith	Black Lace	Yes

Fig. 12. Sample submissions record sheet.

Dealing with tax

If you have something published, you'll need to declare your earnings on your tax return. Publishers will record all payments made to you.

You can claim various expenses against the money you earn; but you need to keep receipts, and accurate records. If you post a manuscript to your publisher, note it down as the exact price and don't round it up (for example, 97p, not £1.00). Ask for receipts each time you purchase anything to do with your writing.

As well as postage costs, you can also claim the cost of:

- travel (for example, to an erotic writers' conference)

- reference books (for example, *Writers' and Artists' Yearbook* and dictionaries)

- telephone calls (for example, to an agent or a publisher)

- paper

- pens, typewriter ribbons, printer cartridges, floppy disks, correction fluid, folders, envelopes, labels and other stationery

- correspondence courses

- subscriptions to relevant publications (for example *Writers News*)

- your accountant's fees.

Your local Inland Revenue office will give you details of self-employed tax allowances; for example, you may be able to claim part of the cost of lighting and heating your house, if you work from home.

You may prefer to leave this in the hands of your accountant. If you choose to use an accountant, ask for quotes from several different firms, and always ask if they've had experience of working with authors.

CHECKLIST

- Make sure that you keep a record of how much you've earned from writing during the last tax year.

- Make sure that you keep a record of how much you've spent on writing-related purchases during the last tax year.

- Keep all your receipts, bank account statements and remittance advices together.

- Keep records of submissions and results and use notes of your rejections to help improve your writing.

CASE STUDY

Zoe keeps up to date

Zoe keeps separate accounts sheets for each category of expenditure, and keeps her receipts in plastic wallets – including remittance advice notes from her publisher. At the end of her tax year, all her records are in order and she feels confident that her tax return is accurate, thus avoiding potential administration problems.

Answers to Assignments

PUNCTUATION

The following is the correctly punctuated passage from page 36.

'I can't believe it's so hot, today,' Jennifer said, reclining on the blanket and stretching.

'The weather man did say that it was going to be nearly 30 degrees – the hottest day of the year,' Sally reminded her friend.

'Yes.' Jennifer mopped her face with a tissue and pushed her dark hair back from her face. 'But I haven't trusted weather forecasts since we held that barbecue last year. It was supposed to be sunny and it rained buckets, remember?'

'Never mind. This,' Sally told her, pouring a glass of pinot noir rosé and handing it to her, 'will make you feel a bit better.'

Jennifer accepted the wine. 'What'd make me feel better is having our own private swimming pool.'

'With Fox Mulder as the lifeguard,' Sally added, a look of sheer lust brightening her eyes.

Jennifer pulled a face. 'That's highly likely, isn't it?'

'About as likely as fitting a swimming pool into our back garden,' Sally retorted, eyeing the narrow courtyard.

Glossary

Blurb The working for the back of the book-jacket; the aim of the blurb is to give an idea of the plot (without giving too much away) and a sample of the writing, usually including a piece of dialogue, to attract readers to buy the book.

Chapter Section of a book, normally numbered but may also have its own title as well.

Conflict The obstacles which the lead character in your novel has to overcome. Usually some form of problem, either practical or emotional.

Contract The legal agreement between you and a publisher stating the title, approximate word-count, delivery date and publication of your novel, plus payment terms.

Copy-editor The person employed by the publishing house to go through your manuscript and check it for house style, factual mistakes and grammatical/spelling errors.

Copyright The legal ownership of publication rights in a piece of written work.

Covering letter A brief letter to an editor asking if he or she will consider publishing your novel.

Dialect The accent or vocabulary used in a particular region rather than nationally.

Dialogue Speech between two or more characters.

Double spacing Manuscript presentation where a blank line is left between each typed line on a page.

Dream-sequence Scene in a novel which turns out to be a dream.

Editor The person at a publishing house who is responsible for commissioning a novel.

Editorial guidelines Information for authors about the publisher's requirements in style, length and content.

Episodic tale A novel where each chapter tells a different story, linked to the preceding and following chapters.

Erotica A short story or novel containing explicit sex scenes, written with the aim of making the reader feel turned on.

Fetish Non-sexual object or part of the body which is endowed with sexual symbolism (for example, gloves and shoes) and arouses sexual excitement.

Flashback A method of revealing past events to shed light on a character's motivation.

Flow diagram The plot of your novel shown in diagrammatic form, with events placed in boxes and connected by lines.

Genre fiction A story or novel which fits into a particular literary category, such as thrillers, crime novels or romance.

House style How a particular publishing house likes things set out – for example, ending past participles such as 'learned' as 'learnt', having dialogue within single speech marks, and the layout of a chapter.

Imprint The name of the 'list' within a publishing house which is under the control of a particular editor. For example, Liaisons is an imprint of Headline, which is a publishing house.

Interaction or interplay The way your characters react to other characters and the setting in your novel.

Lead time The time between the date you deliver the manuscript and the date when the book is finally published.

List The titles published by a publisher.

Plot The events in a story.

Power games The interaction between characters based on the balance of power between them – often in the form of master/ mistress scenarios.

Prelim page A page at the front of the book which contains a short extract of up to ten lines from the novel, aiming to whet the reader's interest.

Proofreader Person employed by the publishers to check proofs for errors.

Proofs Unbound typeset copy of your manuscript.

Pseudonym A name which you may wish to adopt as your writing name.

Rejection letter A letter from an editor saying that your manuscript is not suitable for their imprint. May contain good advice to help you improve your writing.

Romance A short story or novel based around the love affair between two characters, ending with the happy resolution of the conflict between the characters.

Scene Part of a chapter with its own distinct action. There may be more than one scene per chapter.

Set piece A sex scene which is commonly found in an erotic novel.

Setting Where the action in a book takes place, when (contemporary or historical plus the time of year/time of day) and the 'world' in which the characters move.

Slush pile A collection of unsolicited manuscripts.

SM Sadism and masochism; sometimes interpreted as submission and mastery.

Synopsis A brief resume of the characters, setting and plot of your novel.

Targeting Researching and producing work for the specific style of a publishing house.

Throat-clearing In dialogue, when characters say 'Mm' or 'Oh' or 'Well' before a speech.

Timescale The period of time which your novel covers.

Unsolicited manuscript A novel submitted to an editor on speculation.

Vanilla sex Sexual activity which doesn't include bondage, corporal punishment or the use of anything 'kinky'.

Viewpoint The point of view from which your story is told.

Word-count The number of words required by the publisher.

Writer's block A temporary feeling that you are unable to continue writing your novel.

Useful Addresses

ASSOCIATIONS

Guild of Erotic Writers, CTCK, PO Box 8431, London SE8 4BP.
Tel: (0973) 767086

Society of Authors, 84 Drayton Gardens, London SW10 9SB. Tel:
(0171) 373 6642

Women Writers' Network, 55 Burlington Lane, London W4 3ET.
Tel: (0181) 994 0598

Writers' Guild of Great Britain, 430 Edgware Road, London W2
1EH. Tel: (0171) 723 8074

PUBLISHERS OF EROTIC NOVELS

Black Lace, Virgin Publishing Ltd, 332 Ladbroke Grove, London
W10 5AH. *Editor*: Kerri Sharp

Chimera Publishing, PO Box 152, Waterlooville, Hants PO8 9FS.
Editor: Adrian Wilkins

Headline, 338 Euston Road, London NW1 3BH. *Editor*: Mike
Bailey

NEL, 338 Euston Road, London NW1 3BH. *Editor*: Jon Wood

Nexus, Virgin Publishing Ltd, 332 Ladbroke Grove, London W10
5AH. *Editor*: Peter Darvill-Evans

Olympia Publishing, 36 Union Street, Ryde, Isle of Wight PO33
2LE. *Editor*: Josephine Scott

X Libris, Little, Brown & Co, Brettenham House, Lancaster Place,
London WC2E 7EN. *Editor*: Helen Pisano

Further Reading

REFERENCE BOOKS

General
Cassell Spelling Dictionary, Cassell.
Collins English Spelling Dictionary, HarperCollins.
Collins Thesaurus, Collins.
The Writer's Handbook, Macmillan.
Writers' & Artists' Yearbook A & C Black.
Slang down the ages, Jonathon Green, Kyle Cathie Ltd.

EROTIC WRITING

Writing Erotic Fiction, Derek Parker, A&C Black.
The Sexential Guide to Writing Erotic Literature, Josephine Scott, Olympia Press.
Teach Yourself Writing Erotic Writing, Mike Bailey, Hodder & Stoughton.
Sex A to Z, Goldenson & Anderson, World Almanac (also published as Wordsworth's 'Dictionary of Sex').
The New Joy of Sex, Alex Comfort, Mitchell Beazley.
My Secret Garden, Nancy Friday, Quartet Books.

HOW TO BOOKS IN THE SUCCESSFUL WRITING SERIES

Creative Writing, Adèle Ramet.
Copyright and Law for Writers, Helen Shay.
Starting to Write, Marina & Deborah Oliver.
Writing and Selling a Novel, Marina Oliver.
Writing for Publication, Chriss McCallum (4th edition).
Writing Romantic Fiction, Marina Oliver, with a foreword by Joanna Trollope.

Index

COPYRIGHT & LAW FOR WRITERS
How to protect yourself and your creative work

Helen Shay

This book will be a useful tool for any writer, but especially invaluable to beginners and those just starting to enjoy some success. Make sure you never receive any legal short change. This book takes you through the main legal implications relevant to writers, from first putting pen to paper/finger to keyboard through to selling work, entering a contract and onto collecting the full financial rewards due to you. It also explains exactly what to do if things go wrong. It explains the various pitfalls and how to steer clear of them – for example – copyright infringement – whilst showing how to preserve your own rights, and how to publish and not be damned. A graduate of Manchester University, Helen Shay is a qualified solicitor of fourteen years' standing. Currently working in an ombudsman's office in London, she is well-versed in the problems which can confront the individual versus the large organisations. She has also tutored and lectured part-time in business law. She is a member of the Society of Women Writers and Journalists and the Women Writers Network, and currently writes a regular legal column for *Writers News*.

96pp. illus. 1 85703 416 3.

STARTING TO WRITE
How to create written work for publication and profit

Marina & Deborah Oliver

How does a writer get started? How do writers manage the physical aspects? This new book shows would-be writers how to look at their motives, how to set realistic objectives, and how to devise a plan of action without wasting time and resources. Illustrated throughout with case studies, it will show you how to explore various options, discover what methods work best for you, and take advantage of tips from experienced writers. Start now, and learn how to get your work into print. Marina Oliver has written and published over 30 novels, published her own magazine, written and edited many booklets, and taught creative writing. Deborah Oliver had edited a monthly magazine and currently production editor of a computer magazine.

124pp. illus. 1 85703 401 5.

How To Books

How To Books provide practical help on a large range of topics. They are available through all good bookshops or can be ordered direct from the distributors. Just tick the titles you want and complete the form on the following page.

___ Apply to an Industrial Tribunal (£7.99)
___ Applying for a Job (£8.99)
___ Applying for a United States Visa (£15.99)
___ Backpacking Round Europe (£8.99)
___ Be a Freelance Journalist (£8.99)
___ Be a Freelance Secretary (£8.99)
___ Become a Freelance Sales Agent (£9.99)
___ Becoming a Father (£8.99)
___ Buy & Run a Shop (£8.99)
___ Buy & Run a Small Hotel (£8.99)
___ Buying a Personal Computer (£9.99)
___ Career Networking (£8.99)
___ Career Planning for Women (£8.99)
___ Cash from your Computer (£9.99)
___ Choosing a Nursing Home (£9.99)
___ Choosing a Package Holiday (£8.99)
___ Claim State Benefits (£9.99)
___ Collecting a Debt (£9.99)
___ Communicate at Work (£7.99)
___ Conduct Staff Appraisals (£7.99)
___ Conducting Effective Interviews (£8.99)
___ Coping with Self Assessment (£9.99)
___ Copyright & Law for Writers (£8.99)
___ Counsel People at Work (£7.99)
___ Creating a Twist in the Tale (£8.99)
___ Creative Writing (£9.99)
___ Critical Thinking for Students (£8.99)
___ Dealing with a Death in the Family (£9.99)
___ Do Your Own Advertising (£8.99)
___ Do Your Own PR (£8.99)
___ Doing Business Abroad (£10.99)
___ Doing Business on the Internet (£12.99)
___ Doing Voluntary Work Abroad (£9.99)
___ Emigrate (£9.99)
___ Employ & Manage Staff (£8.99)
___ Find Temporary Work Abroad (£8.99)
___ Finding a Job in Canada (£9.99)
___ Finding a Job in Computers (£8.99)
___ Finding a Job in New Zealand (£9.99)
___ Finding a Job with a Future (£8.99)
___ Finding Work Overseas (£9.99)
___ Freelance DJ-ing (£8.99)
___ Freelance Teaching & Tutoring (£9.99)
___ Get a Job Abroad (£10.99)
___ Get a Job in Europe (£9.99)
___ Get a Job in France (£9.99)
___ Get a Job in Travel & Tourism (£8.99)
___ Get into Radio (£8.99)
___ Getting a Job in America (£10.99)
___ Getting a Job in Australia (£9.99)
___ Getting into Films & Television (£10.99)
___ Getting That Job (£8.99)
___ Getting your First Job (£8.99)
___ Going to University (£8.99)
___ Having a Baby (£8.99)

___ Helping your Child to Read (£8.99)
___ How to Study & Learn (£8.99)
___ Investing in People (£9.99)
___ Investing in Stocks & Shares (£9.99)
___ Keep Business Accounts (£7.99)
___ Know Your Rights at Work (£8.99)
___ Learning to Counsel (£9.99)
___ Live & Work in Germany (£9.99)
___ Live & Work in Greece (£9.99)
___ Live & Work in Italy (£8.99)
___ Live & Work in Portugal (£9.99)
___ Live & Work in the Gulf (£9.99)
___ Living & Working in America (£12.99)
___ Living & Working in Australia (£12.99)
___ Living & Working in Britain (£8.99)
___ Living & Working in China (£9.99)
___ Living & Working in Hong Kong (£10.99)
___ Living & Working in Israel (£10.99)
___ Living & Work in New Zealand (£9.99)
___ Living & Working in Saudi Arabia (£12.99)
___ Living & Working in the Netherlands (£9.99)
___ Living Away From Home (£8.99)
___ Making a Complaint (£8.99)
___ Making a Video (£9.99)
___ Making a Wedding Speech (£8.99)
___ Manage a Sales Team (£8.99)
___ Manage an Office (£8.99)
___ Manage Computers at Work (£8.99)
___ Manage People at Work (£8.99)
___ Manage Your Career (£8.99)
___ Managing Budgets & Cash Flows (£9.99)
___ Managing Credit (£8.99)
___ Managing Meetings (£8.99)
___ Managing Projects (£8.99)
___ Managing Your Personal Finances (£8.99)
___ Managing Yourself (£8.99)
___ Market Yourself (£8.99)
___ Mastering Book-Keeping (£8.99)
___ Mastering Business English (£8.99)
___ Master GCSE Accounts (£8.99)
___ Master Public Speaking (£8.99)
___ Migrating to Canada (£12.99)
___ Obtaining Visas & Work Permits (£9.99)
___ Organising Effective Training (£9.99)
___ Passing Exams Without Anxiety (£8.99)
___ Passing That Interview (£8.99)
___ Plan a Wedding (£8.99)
___ Planning Your Gap Year (£8.99)
___ Preparing a Business Plan (£8.99)
___ Publish a Book (£9.99)
___ Publish a Newsletter (£9.99)
___ Raise Funds & Sponsorship (£7.99)
___ Rent & Buy Property in France (£9.99)
___ Rent & Buy Property in Italy (£9.99)
___ Research Methods (£8.99)

___ Retire Abroad (£8.99)	___ Winning Consumer Competitions (£8.99)
___ Return to Work (£7.99)	___ Winning Presentations (£8.99)
___ Run a Voluntary Group (£8.99)	___ Work from Home (£8.99)
___ Setting up Home in Florida (£9.99)	___ Work in an Office (£7.99)
___ Setting Up Your Own Limited Company	___ Work in Retail (£8.99)
(£9.99)	___ Work with Dogs (£8.99)
___ Spending a Year Abroad (£8.99)	___ Working Abroad (£14.99)
___ Start a Business from Home (£7.99)	___ Working as a Holiday Rep (£9.99)
___ Start a New Career (£6.99)	___ Working as an Au Pair (£8.99)
___ Starting to Manage (£8.99)	___ Working in Japan (£10.99)
___ Starting to Write (£8.99)	___ Working in Photography (£8.99)
___ Start Word Processing (£8.99)	___ Working in the Gulf (£10.99)
___ Start Your Own Business (£8.99)	___ Working in Hotels & Catering (£9.99)
___ Study Abroad (£8.99)	___ Working on Contract Worldwide (£9.99)
___ Study & Live in Britain (£7.99)	___ Working on Cruise Ships (£9.99)
___ Studying at University (£8.99)	___ Write a Press Release (£9.99)
___ Studying for a Degree (£8.99)	___ Write & Sell Computer Software (£9.99)
___ Successful Grandparenting (£8.99)	___ Write for Television (£8.99)
___ Successful Mail Order Marketing (£9.99)	___ Writing a CV that Works (£8.99)
___ Successful Single Parenting (£8.99)	___ Writing a Non Fiction Book (£9.99)
___ Survive Divorce (£8.99)	___ Writing a Report (£8.99)
___ Surviving Redundancy (£8.99)	___ Writing a Textbook (£12.99)
___ Taking in Students (£8.99)	___ Writing an Assignment (£8.99)
___ Taking on Staff (£8.99)	___ Writing an Essay (£8.99)
___ Taking Your A-Levels (£8.99)	___ Writing & Publishing Poetry (£9.99)
___ Teach Abroad (£8.99)	___ Writing & Selling a Novel (£8.99)
___ Teach Adults (£8.99)	___ Writing Business Letters (£8.99)
___ Teaching Someone to Drive (£8.99)	___ Writing for Publication (£8.99)
___ Travel Round the World (£8.99)	___ Writing Reviews (£9.99)
___ Understand Finance at Work (£8.99)	___ Writing Romantic Fiction (£9.99)
___ Use a Library (£7.99)	___ Writing Science Fiction (£9.99)
___ Using the Internet (£9.99)	___ Writing Your Dissertation (£8.99)

To: Plymbridge Distributors Ltd, Plymbridge House, Estover Road, Plymouth PL6 7PZ.
Customer Services Tel: (01752) 202301. Fax: (01752) 202331.

Please send me copies of the titles I have indicated. Please add postage & packing
(UK £1, Europe including Eire, £2, World £3 airmail).

☐ I enclose cheque/PO payable to Plymbridge Distributors Ltd for £ _____

☐ Please charge to my ☐ MasterCard, ☐ Visa, ☐ AMEX card.

Account No. [ ][ ][ ][ ][ ][ ][ ][ ][ ][ ][ ][ ][ ][ ][ ][ ]

Card Expiry Date [ ][ ] 19 ☎ **Credit Card orders may be faxed or phoned.**

Customer Name (CAPITALS) ....

Address ....

.... Postcode...............

Telephone........................... Signature ....

Every effort will be made to despatch your copy as soon as possible but to avoid possible
disappointment please allow up to 21 days for despatch time (42 days if overseas). Prices
and availability are subject to change without notice.

Code BPA